Consumer Behaviour in Hospitality and Tourism

Consumer behaviour includes individual decision-making (IDM). IDM has implications in customer satisfaction, loyalty, and other behavioural intentions toward the organisations' products and services. *Consumer Behaviour in Hospitality and Tourism* targets to study consumers and tourists in different leisure and touristic places such as hotels, convention centres, amusement parks, national parks, and the transportation sector.

The aim of this book is to provide a broad view of novel topics and presents the current scenario in the hospitality and business arena. This edited volume has seven chapters and each chapter addresses varied themes relating to consumer behaviour, ranging from sustainable tourism, environmental issues, and green tourism to the impact of hotel online reviews using social media. It will be of great interest to researchers and scholars interested in Consumer Behaviour, Hospitality, and Tourism.

The chapters in this book were originally published as a special issue of the *Journal of Global Scholars of Marketing Science*.

Saurabh Kumar Dixit is Associate Professor and founding Head of the Department of Tourism and Hotel Management, North-Eastern Hill University, Shillong (Meghalaya), India. His research interests include Consumer Behaviour, Gastronomic Tourism, and Experiential Management and Marketing in hospitality and tourism contexts. He has twelve books to his credit. His recent profile can be seen at www.routledge.com/authors/i15903-saurabh-dixit

Kuan-Huei Lee is Associate Professor at Singapore Institute of Technology. She graduated with a PhD in Tourism Management from the University of Queensland, Australia. Her research interests include Food Tourism, Food and Beverage Management, and Cross-cultural Studies of Tourists.

Poh Theng Loo is Assistant Professor at I-Shou University. She graduated with a PhD in Hospitality and Tourism from Taylor's University, Malaysia. Her research interests include any topics of Consumer Behaviour and Services Marketing in tourism and hospitality.

"Consumer Behaviour in Hospitality and Tourism is a concerted collection of studies featuring strategies and tips to better engage the community as consumers, predict customer brand trust, evaluate official destination websites, implement green hotel practices, increase positive sentiment reviews for hotels, improve consumer recycling behaviours during vacations, and measure visitor satisfaction from ecotourism experiences. The book editors, Saurabh K. Dixit, Kuan-Huei Lee, and Poh Theng Loo, have highlighted interesting hospitality and tourism cases, including how one tourism site became the cleanest village in Asia!"

Catheryn Khoo - Lattimore, Ph.D., Multi-award-winning Tourism Researcher and Consultant to the UNWTO

"I found the book interesting to read. I learned many different tourism practices, especially the topic of green marketing and recycling behaviour on vacation. The book is a much-awaited contribution complied with contemporary issues that offer updated knowledge in the area of consumer behaviour. It offers a variety of cutting edge and current topics while exploring relevant practical examples supported by sound theoretical contributions and critical debates. I recommend this book and believe it is a key reference for researchers, lecturers, and students, and it is also an essential read for others keen to learn more about consumer behaviour in tourism."

Xiang Ying MEI, Ph.D., Inland Norway University of Applied Sciences, Norway

"The book covers several pertinent topics that are attracting important attention in the field of consumer behaviour in tourism, ranging from assessment of performance, guest hospitality assessment, brand identification, green marketing, local community engagement, and recycling behaviour. The title appears quite interesting and enabling learners to have insights into different facets of consumer behaviour of hospitality and tourism."

Sari Lenggogeni, Ph.D., Universitas, Andalas, Indonesia

Consumer Behaviour in Hospitality and Tourism

Edited by
Saurabh Kumar Dixit, Kuan-Huei Lee, and Poh Theng Loo

Routledge
Taylor & Francis Group

LONDON AND NEW YORK

First published 2022
by Routledge
2 Park Square, Milton Park, Abingdon, Oxon OX14 4RN

and by Routledge
605 Third Avenue, New York, NY 10158

Routledge is an imprint of the Taylor & Francis Group, an informa business

British Library Cataloguing in Publication Data
A catalogue record for this book is available from the British Library

ISBN: 978-1-032-01934-5 (hbk)
ISBN: 978-1-032-01936-9 (pbk)
ISBN: 978-1-003-18107-1 (ebk)

DOI: 10.4324/9781003181071

Typeset in Minion Pro
by Newgen Publishing UK

Publisher's Note
The publisher accepts responsibility for any inconsistencies that may have arisen during the conversion of this book from journal articles to book chapters, namely the inclusion of journal terminology.

Disclaimer
Every effort has been made to contact copyright holders for their permission to reprint material in this book. The publishers would be grateful to hear from any copyright holder who is not here acknowledged and will undertake to rectify any errors or omissions in future editions of this book.

Contents

Citation Information

The chapters in this book were originally published in the *Journal of Global Scholars of Marketing Science*, volume 29, issue 2 (2019). When citing this material, please use the original page numbering for each article, as follows:

Chapter 1
Consumer behavior in hospitality and tourism
Saurabh Kumar Dixit, Kuan-Huei Lee and Poh Theng Loo
Journal of Global Scholars of Marketing Science, volume 29, issue 2 (2019), pp. 151–161

Chapter 2
Visitors' satisfaction from ecotourism in the protected area of the Indian Himalayan Region using importance–performance analysis
Priya Bhalla and Prodyut Bhattacharya
Journal of Global Scholars of Marketing Science, volume 29, issue 2 (2019), pp. 162–179

Chapter 3
How user-generated judgments of hotel attributes indicate guest satisfaction
Sangeetha Gunasekar and Sooriya Sudhakar
Journal of Global Scholars of Marketing Science, volume 29, issue 2 (2019), pp. 180–195

Chapter 4
Customer brand identification, affective commitment, customer satisfaction, and brand trust as antecedents of customer behavioral intention of loyalty: An empirical study in the hospitality sector
Raouf Ahmad Rather, Shehnaz Tehseen, Murtaza Hassan Itoo and Shakir Hussain Parrey
Journal of Global Scholars of Marketing Science, volume 29, issue 2 (2019), pp. 196–217

Chapter 5
Hotel's best practices as strategic drivers for environmental sustainability and green marketing
Chindu Chandran and Prodyut Bhattacharya
Journal of Global Scholars of Marketing Science, volume 29, issue 2 (2019), pp. 218–233

For any permission-related enquiries please visit:
www.tandfonline.com/page/help/permissions

Notes on Contributors

Stefanie Benjamin, Department of Retail, Hospitality & Tourism Management, University of Tennessee, Knoxville, TN, USA.

Priya Bhalla, University School of Environment Management, Guru Gobind Singh Indraprastha University, New Delhi, India.

Prodyut Bhattacharya, University School of Environment Management, Guru Gobind Singh Indraprastha University, New Delhi, India.

Chindu Chandran, University School of Environment Management, Guru Gobind Singh Indraprastha University, New Delhi, India.

Saurabh Kumar Dixit, Department of Tourism & Hotel Management, North-Eastern Hill University, Shillong, India.

Sangeetha Gunasekar, Amrita School of Business, Amrita Vishwa Vidyapeetham, Coimbatore, India.

Murtaza Hassan Itoo, The Business School, University of Jammu, Jammu and Kashmir, India.

Kuan-Huei Lee, Design and Specialised Businesses Cluster, Singapore Institute of Technology, Singapore.

Hillary Leonard, College of Business, University of Rhode Island – College of Pharmacy, Kingston, RI, USA.

Poh Theng Loo, International Tourism and Hospitality Department, I-Shou University, Kaohsiung City, Taiwan.

Jason Oliver, Gabelli School of Business, Roger Williams University, Bristol, RI, USA.

Shakir Hussain Parrey, Department of Management studies, South Campus, University of Kashmir, Srinagar, India.

Raouf Ahmad Rather, The Business School, University of Jammu, Jammu and Kashmir, India.

Bijoylaxmi Sarmah, Centre for Management Studies, North-Eastern Regional Institute of Science & Technology, Itanagar, India.

Harshada Rajeev Satghare, Department of Tourism Administration, Babasaheb Ambedkar Marathwada University, Aurangabad, Maharashtra, India.

Madhuri Sawant, Department of Tourism Administration, Babasaheb Ambedkar Marathwada University, Aurangabad, Maharashtra, India.

Neeraj Sharma, Department of Management Studies, Indian Institute of Technology Roorkee, Roorkee, India.

Sooriya Sudhakar, Amrita School of Business, Amrita Vishwa Vidyapeetham, Coimbatore, India.

Shehnaz Tehseen, Sunway University Business School, Sunway University, Bandar Sunway, Malaysia.

Consumer behavior in hospitality and tourism

Saurabh Kumar Dixit (ID), Kuan-Huei Lee (ID), and Poh Theng Loo (ID)

ABSTRACT

Consumer behavior includes individual decision-making (IDM). IDM has implications in customer satisfaction, loyalty and other behavioral intentions toward the organizations' products and services. Consumer behavior in hospitality and tourism targets to study consumers and tourists in different leisure and touristic places such as hotels, convention centers, amusement parks, national parks and the transportation sector. This present special issue of JGSMS on the "Consumer Behavior in Hospitality and Tourism" applies an interdisciplinary approach in the selection of papers. The aim is to provide a broad view of novel topics and presents the current scenario in the hospitality and business arena. After exhausting double-blind peer review process, the issue includes seven papers. These papers address varied themes relating to consumer behavior ranging from sustainable tourism, environmental issues and green tourism to the impact of hotel online reviews using social media.

酒店业与旅游业中的消费者行为

消费者行为包括个人决策。个人决策对客户满意度、忠诚度和其他对各个组织产品和服务的行为意图方面有影响。酒店和旅游中的消费者行为旨在研究不同休闲和旅游场所的消费者和游客，如酒店、会议中心、游乐园、国家公园和交通部门。本期《全球营销科学学报》特刊主题为"酒店和旅游业中的消费者行为"，在论文选择中采用了跨学科的方法。其目的在于给各类新颖主题提供更为广泛的见解，并且展现出酒店业和商业领域的现状。经过穷尽的双盲审程序后，本期特刊选取了七篇论文。这七篇论文解决了与消费者行为有关的各类主题，从可持续旅游业、环保旅游业、绿色旅游业到使用社交媒体的酒店在线评论所带来的影响。

Introduction

Hospitality and tourism studies are the emerging disciplines where the body of knowledge is evolving with the advancements in the society, culture and human behavior (Dixit, 2018). The study of consumer behavior touches almost every aspect of our daily lives. The origin of consumer behavior literature can be traced back to 1960s, to respond the increasing demand to find a better market segmentation base by segmenting people based on their values (Veal, 1991). In today's digital and modern world, consumer behavior may be the central theme to understand the key facets of our changing lifestyles. The need for the marketer to be flexible and adaptable to the changing world around them has never been so robust. As competition in the market intensifies and consumers become more demanding from the suppliers, marketers must be increasingly sensitive to a multitude of sociocultural distinctions.

Consumer behavior is a process that involves a transaction where two or more parties (organization or person) give and receive something of value (Solomon, 2015). Consumer behavior has been defined by Blackwell, Miniard and Engel (2001) as "those activities directly involved in obtaining, consuming, and disposing of products and services including the decision processes that precedes and follows these actions". This definition emphasizes the importance of psychological process that consumer goes through during the prepurchase, purchase and post-purchase stages. The conceptual understanding of consumer behavior would be helpful and worthwhile for marketers to identify ways to develop their marketing and promotional strategies in order to offer better quality of products and services.

Consumer behavior is associated to individual decision-making. The traditional view of decision-making process of the consumers involves five steps such as problem recognition, information search, judgment, decision-making and post-decision processes. Once the buying decision is made and the desired item is purchased, it leads to the final step in the decision-making process, which involves evaluating the outcome. It has implications for customer satisfaction, loyalty and other behavioral intentions toward the organizations.

There are four factors that influence the decision process of a consumer: internal, external, situational and marketing-mix. First, *internal factors* are related to the cognitive psychology and deal with how consumers receive information from the environment, process and store them. In order to accumulate information, researchers opt for the amalgamation of the internal and external information sources (Gowreesunkar & Dixit, 2017). The decision-making is influenced by personal value, attitude, perception and personality. Second, *external factors* are those surrounded to the consumer and they are usually related to family members, social class, reference group, culture and subculture of the consumer. Third, *situational factors* are external to the consumer and are factors related to the context such as the mood of the day, time pressure and information searched. Finally, *market factors* refer to the marketing mix of four P's that marketers use to formulate strategies: product, price, place and promotion.

Consumer behavior in hospitality and tourism

Consumer behavior in the arena of hospitality and tourism studies deals with the consumption behavior of guests and tourists. The industrial revolution incentivized the development of lodging and travel industry with Thomas Cook as the initiator of mass tourism in the 19th century, who arranged packaged tours and excursions across Europe. Nowadays, the hospitality and tourism industry involves lodging, event planning, theme parks, transportation, cruise lines, travel agency and food and beverage businesses among others.

The study of consumer behavior in hospitality and tourism includes pre-visit, on-site and post-visit of the tourists to the particular destination. One way of conducting consumer research in hospitality and tourism is through psychographics. Psychographics influence an individual's everyday routine, activities, interests, opinions, values, needs and perceptions. Consumer research in this area is usually linked with using surveys and analytical studies focus mainly on values, attitudes and market segmentation of the target population. Psychographic variables are useful to identify and segment market. Psychographics register people's activities (what they do), interests (what they want) and opinions (what they think). Segmentation by psychographic includes age, gender, family structure, social class and income, race and ethnicity, geography and lifestyles. It is common in the hospitality and tourism literate studies trying to understanding guests, visitors and tourists of a particular venue or destination using psychographic segmentation.

Storytelling is another widely used tool in the marketing of hospitality and tourism products. Storytelling is a powerful way of transmitting ideas to the desired person and through narrative of the story. It can assist in the development of many emotional touchpoints to fulfill intangible sentiments that are core human needs. Storytelling is also a useful marketing tool that targets consumer's emotion, evoke action, create value and easy to remember by the consumer. People who can relate to the story are stimulated to remember more and react to the feelings awakened by the story (Woodside, Sood, & Miller, 2008). Storytelling could be the best tool to engage with tourists and communicate values, history, tradition and common practices of a destination that they visit.

Stages of consumer behavior in hospitality and tourism

In existing literature, researchers have proposed different models of stages of consumer behavior. One of the models is introduced by Aho in 2001, which is related to tourism experience. This dynamic model of tourism experiences consists of a series of seven stages of experience reflecting the tourist behavior. The first stage is initiated with *orientation*, which relates to the awakening of interest and expectations in their life for memories, tangible artifacts and practices. The second stage is *attachment* in which tourists strengthen their interest due to the go-decision for the trip. The third stage is the *actual visitation* of destination and consumption of tourism products. Next is *evaluation* of their experiences, tourists making comparisons between their earlier experiences and alternatives and make conclusions for future decisions. This is followed by the fifth stage which is *storing*. Storing can be of three types: social (people and social situation to remember), physical (photos, souvenirs, films) and mental (affections, new meanings and impressions). The final two stages, sixth and seventh, are *reflection* and *enrichment*. *Reflection* is the repeated presentations of their experiences either by spontaneous and staged. Lastly, *enrichment* is the presentations of photos, souvenirs, arrangement of meetings and networks to cherish memories of trips.

The rapid development of technology in the past decade has influenced the overall consumption process of tourists. Social media, or Web 2.0 as it is popularly known as, has changed drastically the visitor behavior. People have different consumption behavior before, during and after visiting a place. Awareness in eco-tourism, online reviews, social media, big data, Internet of Things and block chain are disrupting the traditional way of consumption.

With the introduction of smart phones, social media and its diverse applications are the main source of communication and information sharing. Applications such as Facebook, Twitter and Instagram are mediums used to share opinions, reviews about products and interact with other users. Social media is one of the most efficient ways to spread messages across, as it is free and reachable within a few clicks. Four out of five brands now utilize Twitter as a tool of marketing while 65% of small business owners claimed that social media has helped them stay connected with their customers. Since social media has succeeded in making users to be attractive, it has become one of the powerful tools in giving and getting reviews (Leung, Law, van Hoof, & Buhalis, 2013). This kind of sharing is also known as electronic word of mouth (eWOM); consumers nowadays have the habit of sharing own experiences of travels, food and service opinions. These microblogging sites could be the best platforms to attain instant feedbacks which have the potential to influence future consumers (Gupta & Harris, 2010).

The advancement of technology promotes the emergence of online review website such as Trip Advisor, Booking.com, Hotels.com, Expedia.com and social media such as Facebook and Instagram have substantial roles and impacts on tourists' purchase behavior, especially their pre purchase and post-purchase experiences. Tourists tend to rely heavily on user-generated contents (social media, blogs, online review websites, online communities) to minimize their risks of purchase. The user-generated contents have critical roles in tourist information search and travel behavior beyond as a source of information; indeed, these contents are recognized as part of the tourists' information search process (Cox, Burgess, Sellitto, & Buultjens, 2009). According to Leung, Law, Hoof and Buhalis (2013), they extensively reviewed literature on social media and highlighted many previous studies on consumer-focused studies on the use and impact of social media in the research stage of tourists' travel planning process. This finding is supported by an empirical study which pointed out that social media is predominantly used by tourists as primary source of information for travel planning for upcoming trips (Xiang, Magnini, & Fesenmaier, 2015).

Consumer behavior stages in services context cover *pre purchase, service encounter and post-purchase* (Wirtz, Chew, & Lovelock, 2012). Wirtz and his colleagues categorized service consumption into three main stages in which each stage comprises performances to be done by consumers or service providers. For instance, at the first stage of service consumption model, *prepurchase stage* begins with the need awareness, information search, evaluation of alternatives to deciding whether to purchase the product or service or not. Under the evaluation of alternatives, consumers should consider the risks involved in purchasing and using the services. There are seven types of perceived risks: (1) functional risk (unsatisfactory performance outcomes), (2) financial risk (monetary loss, unexpected costs), (3) temporal (waste of time due to delays), (4) physical risk (personal injury or damage to belongings), (5) psychological risk (personal fear and emotions), (6) social risk (how others think and react toward purchaser) and sensory risk (unwanted effects on any of the five senses).

Consumer behavior in hospitality and tourism has some unique aspects as this industry consists of many intangible service elements throughout the three main stages. For example, tourist purchases a travel package or books a hotel room that can be considered as an investment with no tangible rate of return and the purchase is usually prepared and planned through careful thoughts and savings made over a period of time (Moutinho, 1987). Due to the unique service characteristics (perishability, inseparability, intangible, heterogeneity), tourists tend to be even more careful and they have greater perceived risks awareness to ensure their purchases in their trips are value for money and memorable. To minimize the risks of purchase and maximize the values gain from the service experience in trips, undeniably, tourists will make their best effort to have a well plan for trips. Hence, technology plays critical roles in facilitating tourists' purchase experiences. For instance, hotel guests or restaurant diners will search online information to evaluate the types of risks involved and making comparison of attributes for brands available prior to making their final purchase decision, which is the final chosen hotel or restaurant brand for subsequent product and service consumption.

Second stage of *service consumption* is service encounter, which refers to customer interaction with service provider directly (Wirtz et al., 2012). Moment of truth is important in managing the touch points during service delivery process. The service encounter process during consumption of service throughout the trip (hotel staying, restaurant dining and destination visitation) is also influenced by the information obtained from the user-generated contents heavily as information collected forms their service expectations throughout the trips. The convenience of smart phone usage is that tourists can browse website information or Facebook pages, blogs and so on to verify the expected information and service to be delivered compared to the actual delivery. Besides that, they can also take pictures and post their comments instantly during the service encounter and service consumption to express their thoughts and mood in social media while consuming the service delivered. They do not need to wait until finishing and leaving the destination or hospitality companies to engage in post-purchase behavior such as word of mouth.

The pre-purchase and service encounter stages have influences on the tourists' later post-purchase outcomes such as behavioral intentions, satisfaction and loyalty. Till today, studies on customer satisfaction and behavioral intentions are still recognized imperative. In particular, industry practitioners need to comprehend if they are able to fulfill or exceed their customer expectations and they would consider revisiting or repurchasing in the future. Customers also tend to share their experiences either via word of mouth or eWOM, which is powerful as this will also affect the tourism and hospitality companies' future sales from other potential or existing customers. Social media is indeed being mainly employed by tourists after holidays for experience sharing and user-generated contents are being perceived as the most trustworthy compared to others such as travel agents, official tourism websites and mass media advertising (Fotis, Buhalis & Rossides, 2012). At this stage, service provider engages with customers the most as they interact face to face during the service delivery and consumption process. If any mistakes occur, service employees can take corrective actions immediately to recover the failure and restore customer satisfaction before leaving the premise and engage in negative post-behavior outcome such as negative word of mouth.

The final stage of consumer service consumption is *post-purchase*. A study revealed that social media has facilitating functions in the social interaction of consumers which lead to the leverage level of trust and intention to purchase (Hajli, 2014). One of the essential tourist behavioral outcomes is satisfaction, which is called a consequence of perceived value (Sanchez, Callarisa, Rodriguez & Moliner, 2006). Moreover, satisfaction or dissatisfaction occurs instantly after the purchase and consumption experience and the post-purchase perceived value is part of customer learning and determines their subsequent attitude of loyalty too. Perceived value of purchasing of tourism products is deemed as a dynamic variable as a single whole experience comprises before purchase, during purchase, at the time of consumption and after consumption (Sanchez et al., 2006). Sanchez et al. (2006) proposed six dimensions of measurement of the perceived overall value of purchase: (1) functional value of travel agency (installations), (2) functional value of the contact personnel of travel agency (professionalism), (3) functional value of the tourism package purchased (quality), (4) functional value prices, (5) emotional value of a purchase and (6) social value of a purchase. Together, all these six dimensions enable industry practitioners to evaluate the tourists' perceived value of their purchase more comprehensively.

Put altogether, the stages of consumer behavior from different research studies, tourism and hospitality industry involve greater personal interaction in service delivery. Therefore, tourism and hospitality companies have to gauge and know well about the tourist behavior in all stages to ensure the success of each service transaction in the business as well as the future business. In particular, investigation on the social media, post-purchase intentions are important as tourism and hospitality companies have to evaluate the service employee service performance meeting the customer expectations and company standards accordingly.

Organization of the book: In this book, an interdisciplinary approach was taken to select chapters to increase the reader's understanding about the theme to address implicit–explicit concerns of consumers' (tourists') behavior. Each of these chapters maps a different facet of the changing world of consumer behavior. Seven chapters included in this book therefore provide a broad overview of current scenario of consumer behavior particularly for hospitality and tourism businesses. In this book, sustainable tourism is one of the most discussed topics. The second important topic is the research on consumers' online reviews. There is an increasing awareness on environment concerns, consumers are also seeking travel behaviors that would not jeopardize the natural environment and follow green consumption practices (Jackson, 2010). Since consumers are changing their demand over time, there is an increasing concern about environmental issues and businesses have developed sustainable ecological friendly products as well as services to meet this demand (Gao & Mattila, 2014).

Assessing performance

The first chapter authored by Priya Bhalla and Prodyut Bhattacharya (2019) assesses the importance and performance of the service and facility attributes offered in order to measure visitor satisfaction from ecotourism experience in the protected area of the Binsar Wildlife Sanctuary (BWLS), located in the Kumaon administrative division of the Uttarakhand State of India by applying Importance-Performance Analysis. The present research suggests that the most important attributes identified by BWLS visitors to measure visitor satisfaction levels were "social space", "visitor safety", "view point conditions", "food quality", "accommodation facility", "environmental conservation" and "user facilities". With respect to perceived performance of sanctuary facilities and service attributes, visitors were most satisfied with "ease of viewing", "species diversity", "local development", "view point conditions" and "environmental conservation". The study subsequently concludes that the interests and expectations of protected area visitors are focused equally on hospitality and logistics, and natural setup.

Guest hospitality assessment

The second chapter authored by Sangeetha Gunasekar and Sooriya Sudhakar (2019) strives to understand the hotel attributes that contribute toward customer satisfaction or dissatisfaction based on online reviews for hotels of Andaman and Nicobar Islands (India). In this study, the text reviews generated for hotels on the TripAdvisor website are used to understand the significant issues that influence the satisfaction and dissatisfaction of hotel consumers. The study further identifies some of the important attributes of the hotels that help to increase positive sentiment of reviews and reduces the impact of the negative reviews. This can further help the hotel managers to improve the facilities provided to tourists.

Customer brand identification

In the third chapter, authored by Raouf Ahmad Rather, Shehnaz Tehseen, Shakir Hussain Parrey and Murtaza Hassan Itoo (2019) portray an integrated model to explore how customer brand identification (CBI), affective commitment, customer satisfaction and brand trust influence the development of customer behavioral intention of loyalty (CBIL) in the hospitality sector. This study delivers two important contributions. *First*, by developing an integrative social identity / relationship marketing-based model, it contributes to the current understanding of the role of key relational concepts, including customer satisfaction, hotel brand trust, affective commitment and CBIL. *Second*, the study provides managerial suggestions on customer retention and loyalty development expected to be useful to (upscale) hotel managers and other stakeholders. Therefore, this paper simultaneously examines the relationships among CBI, affective commitment, customer satisfaction, brand trust and CBIL, having developed and empirically tested an integrated model that comprehensively assessed these relationships. The study provides a valuable instrument for hospitality sector to evaluate the effectiveness of marketing strategies developed to provide superior customer identification, emotional and/or affective commitment, and better behavioral intention of loyalty.

Green marketing practices

Chapter four authored by Chindu Chandran and Prodyut Bhattacharya (2019) focuses on the need of green marketing practices to be adopted in the accommodation units. The chapter describes the benefits and challenges associated with adopting the environmental best practices and integrating these practices into their marketing strategy especially in the hospitality industry. Hence, the authors focus primarily on the roles that the hoteliers can perform in the preservation of the natural environment by incorporating various green practices into their operations and thus highlighting their practices by means of green marketing. Therefore, it is proposed that the accommodation units must adopt appropriate green practices that will give cost benefits in the future and drives income in the long haul. Hotel operators are expected to contribute vitally in educating their consumers to create awareness about green practices as the concept of green marketing is quite new to India.

Website assessment

Fifth chapter authored by Harshada Satghare and Madhuri Sawant (2019) evaluates the official website of Maharashtra Tourism Development Corporation (MTDC), India, through user judgment approach. The researchers employed instrument "Destination website evaluation scale" to measure the website based on five critical success factors, that is, quality of information, ease of use, customization and interactivity, trust and identity building components and online booking. The present study therefore bridges the existing research gap by evaluating the website of MTDC from user's perspective, which will be helpful in understanding visitor behavior, user satisfaction and perceptions relating to the MTDC website.

Local community engagement

In the sixth chapter, Neeraj Sharma and Bijoylaxmi Sarmah (2019) focus on the important issue of local community and consumer engagement, continuity of traditional heritage and education of the village community leading to improved customer experience and satisfaction. Revealing this process occurs in terms of tourism development and economic growth resulted in village community of Mawlynnong, Meghalaya (India). The population for the present study comprised tourists, local village community members, researchers and academicians who are well aware of the tourism potential of Mawlynnong. Results of the present study indicate that traditional and indigenous heritage and education influence customer engagement, which further influences experience, experience leads to customer satisfaction and customer satisfaction finally results in positive behavioral intention.

Recycling behavior

The final chapter by Jason D. Oliver, Stefanie Benjamin and Hillary Leonard (2019) highlights the recycling behavior of individuals on vacations. The paper starts by offering background on environmental values and environmental self-efficacy and their proposed relationships to recycling behavior. The article demonstrates that recycling behavior varies at home and while on vacation with individuals recycling less on vacation. It further examines how individuals' environmental values, self-efficacy, attitudes toward recycling and perceptions that recycling is worth the effort relate to reported recycling frequency on vacation. The article therefore provides the suggestions to improve recycling behaviors for consumers when they are at home and when they are tourists.

Conclusion

The ultimate goal of this title is to accumulate some of the eminent original works in the domain of consumer behavior particularly for hospitality and tourism. The outputs and contents of each chapter of this volume could enhance the existing body of knowledge on consumer behavior. It also offers more insightful findings and triggers new ideas to explore or expand further on the subject of consumer behavior in hospitality and tourism, in particular, in the areas of study on social media and post-purchase behavior of the consumers. In fact, future studies on green marketing and the usage of social media as engagement medium for companies to communicate and engage with the consumers are getting greater attentions and attractions among the academicians and industry practitioners. The post-purchase behaviors undeniably have substantial and imperative influences on consumer future purchase intention and their future purchase behavior. In this global competitive environment, marketing studies and data that are customer-oriented are necessary and critical for better and effective marketing strategies for sustainable profits and businesses. We hope you will enjoy these articles and that they will offer you a perspective on the concerns and distresses relating to the consumer behavior in hospitality and tourism.

Disclosure statement

No potential conflict of interest was reported by the authors.

ORCID

Saurabh Kumar Dixit ⓘ http://orcid.org/0000-0002-9478-084X
Kuan-Huei Lee ⓘ http://orcid.org/0000-0003-4722-109X
Poh Theng Loo ⓘ http://orcid.org/0000-0002-6859-7769

References

Aho, S. K. (2001). Towards a general theory of touristic experiences: Modelling experience process in tourism. *Tourism Review, 56*(3/4), 33–37.

Bhalla, P., & Bhattacharya, P. (2019). Visitors' satisfaction from ecotourism in the protected area of the Indian Himalayan Region using importance–performance analysis. *Journal of Global Scholars of Marketing Science 29*(2), 162–179.

Blackwell, R.D., Miniard, P.W., & Engel, J.F.(2001).*Consumer behavior* (9th ed.). Mason, OH: South-Western Thomas Learning.

Chandran, C., & Bhattacharya, P. (2019). Hotel's best practices as strategic drivers for environmental sustainability and green marketing. *Journal of Global Scholars of Marketing Science 29*(2), 218–233.

Cox, C., Burgess, S., Sellitto, C., & Buultjens, J. (2009). The role of user-generated content in tourists' travel planning behavior. *Journal of Hospitality Marketing & Management, 18*(8), 743–764.

Dixit, S. K. (2018). The Routledge handbook of hospitality studies. *Hospitality &Society, 8*(1), 99–102.

Dixit, S. K., Lee, K-H., & Loo, P. T. (2019). Consumer behavior in hospitality and tourism. *Journal of Global Scholars of Marketing Science 29*(2), 151–161.

Fotis, J. N., & Buhalis, D., & Rossides, N. (2012). Social media use and impact during the holiday travel planning process. In M. Fuchs, F. Ricci & L. Cantoni (Eds.), *Communication Technologies in Tourism 2012* (pp.13–24).Vienna: Springer-Verlag.

Gao, Y. L., & Mattila, A. S. (2014). Improving consumer satisfaction in green hotels s learning. Mason, OH: The roles of perceived warmth, perceived competence, and CSR motive. *International Journal of Hospitality Management, 42*, 20–31.

Gowreesunkar, G., & Dixit, S. (2017). Consumer information-seeking behaviour. In S. Dixit (Ed.), *The Routledge handbook of consumer behaviour in hospitality and tourism* (pp. 55–68). Abingdon: Routledge.

Gunasekar, S., & Sudhakar, S. (2019). How user-generated judgments of hotel attributes indicate guest satisfaction. *Journal of Global Scholars of Marketing Science 29*(2), 180–195.

Gupta, P., & Harris, J. (2010). How e-WOM recommendations influence product consideration and quality of choice: A motivation to process information perspective. *Journal of Business Research, 63*(9–10), 1041–1049.

Hajli, N. M. (2014). A study of the impact of social media on consumers. *International Journal of Market Research, 56*(3), 387–404.

Jackson, L. A. (2010). Toward a framework for the components of green lodging. *Journal of Retail & Leisure Property, 9*(3), 211–230.

Leung, D., Law, R., van Hoof, H., & Buhalis, D. (2013). Social media in tourism and hospitality: A literature review. *Journal of Travel & Tourism Marketing, 30*(1–2), 3–22.

Oliver, J., Benjamin, S., & Leonard, H. (2019). Recycling on vacation: Does pro-environmental behavior change when consumers travel? *Journal of Global Scholars of Marketing Science 29*(2), 266–280.

Rather, R. A., Tehseen, S., Itoo, M. H., & Hussain, S. (2019). Customer brand identification, affective commitment, customer satisfaction, and brand trust as antecedents of customer behavioral intention of loyalty: An empirical study in the hospitality sector. *Journal of Global Scholars of Marketing Science 29*(2), 196–217.

Moutinho, L. (1987). Consumer behaviour in tourism. *European Journal of Marketing, 21*(10), 5–44.

Sa´nchez, J., Callarisa, L., Rodrı´guez, R. M., & Moliner, M. A. (2006). Perceived value of the purchase of a tourism product. *Tourism Management, 27*(2006), 394–409.

Satghare, H. R., Sawant, M. (2019). Evaluation of official destination website of Maharashtra state (India) from the customer perspectives. *Journal of Global Scholars of Marketing Science 29*(2), 234–247.

Sharma, N., & Sarmah, B. (2019). Consumer engagement in village eco-tourism: A case of the cleanest village in Asia – Mawlynnong. *Journal of Global Scholars of Marketing Science 29*(2), 248–265.

Solomon, M. R. (2015). *Consumer behavior: Buying, having, and being* (11th ed.). Harlow: Pearson Education.

Veal, A. J. (1991). *Lifestyle and leisure: A review and bibliography* (Vol. 13). Sydney: Centre for Leisure & Tourism Studies, University of Technology.

Wirtz, J., Chew, P., & Lovelock, C. (2012).Consumer behavior in a services context. In *Essentials of services marketing* (2nd, pp. 34–65). Singapore: Pearson Education.

Woodside, A. G., Sood, S., & Miller, K. E. (2008). When consumers and brands talk: Storytelling theory and research in psychology and marketing. *Psychology & Marketing, 25*(2), 97–145.

Xiang, A. N., Magnini, V. P., & Fesenmaier, D. R. (2015). Information technology and consumer behavior in travel and tourism: Insights from travel planning using the internet. *Journal of Retailing and Consumer Services, 22*(2015), 244–249.

Visitors' satisfaction from ecotourism in the protected area of the Indian Himalayan Region using importance–performance analysis

Priya Bhalla and Prodyut Bhattacharya (iD)

ABSTRACT

Protected areas are increasingly becoming primary focus for eco-tourism. Binsar Wildlife Sanctuary situated in the Indian Himalayan Region offers its visitors key ecotourism products like enjoying Himalayan vistas, nature trekking, bird watching, photography and the homestays. Visitors to ecologically fragile destinations form crucial tourism stakeholders and require understanding of their demands and satisfaction levels to sustain a flow of visitors in the increasingly competitive tourism market. The present research assessed the importance and performance of the service and facilities attributes offered by the sanctuary in order to measure visitor satisfaction from ecotourism experience, using an importance–performance analysis. Findings indicate good performance of service providers in terms of environmental conservation, ensuring safety of visitors and maintaining view point conditions. Whereas, efforts need to be concentrated in improving user facilities, nature guiding, signage and information, food quality, and accommodation facility attributes. Chi-square analysis revealed that visitors undertaking unplanned day visit to the sanctuary were more likely to be non-satisfied, raising questions on the type of visitors arriving at the sanctuary. In order to enhance visitors' satisfaction levels, basic facilities within the sanctuary need improvement besides developing interpretations component, such that the intrinsic nature and quality of nature-based ecotourism destination is achieved.

重要性-绩效分析视角下印度喜马拉雅保护区生态旅游游客满意度

保护区日益成为生态旅游的主要焦点。宾萨尔野生动物保护区（Binsar Wildlife Sanctuary）位于印度喜马拉雅地区，它为游客提供生态旅游产品，主要包括欣赏喜马拉雅山景观、自然徒步旅行、观鸟、摄影和寄宿家庭。到生态脆弱地的游客与旅游业的利益息息相关，了解他们的需求和满意度可以在竞争日益激烈的旅游市场中维持游客的流动量。本研究运用重要性-绩效分析，评估宾萨尔野生动物保护区提供的服务和设施属性的重要性和绩效，以此衡量生态旅游体验的游客满意度。调查结果表明服务供应商在环境保护、保证游客安全和维持动态角度方面表现良好。然而，需要集中精力改善的是用户设施、自然导游、标志和信息、食品质量和住宿设施属性方面。卡方检验对到达保护区的游客类型提出问题，结果显示在保护区进行无计划游玩的游客更有可能感到不满意。为了提高游客的满意度，除了开发解释组件外，保护区内的基础设施还需要改进，体现出自然生态旅游地的内在本质和质量。

Introduction

Ecotourism in protected areas (PA) of mountain destinations is growing rapidly with a huge range of players involved in ecotourism development and management. Strong partnerships among these players', classified broadly under core decision-makers (the PA managers, local communities, tourism industries, government officials and non-governmental organizations) and supporting players (funding agencies, academicians and visitors) often act as a key to the success of ecotourism in terms of achieving biodiversity conservation (Bookbinder, Dinerstein, Rijal, Cauley, & Rajouria, 1998) and equitable development goals (Drumm & Moore, 2005) for any ecotourism destination. Wherein, visitors' inclination for nature and PAs (Hausmann et al., 2018) makes ecotourism a potential tourism market, and subsequently, visitor satisfaction vital to ensure ecotourism's long-term sustainability (Newsome, Rodger, Pearce, & Chan, 2017). Thus, understanding visitors role in ecotourism becomes crucial as the visitors not only provide motivation for other players' activities (Rastogi, Badola, Hussain, & Hickey, 2010), but their destination choice impacts upon the eventual success or failure of ecotourism projects (Drumm & Moore, 2005; Treweek, 1999). Whereas, the PA managers are challenged with the mandate of protecting natural and cultural resources while providing for high-quality, sustainable recreation use (Buckley, 2004, Rastogi et al., 2010; Spenceley, 2008). Further, they are challenged by the issue of achieving this goal with often decreasing budgets (Rome, 1999) and staff, yet increasing visitor numbers (Butler, 1980; Lindberg, Kreg, Stephen, & Stankey, 1997; McCool & Lime, 2000) and increasing competition from other tourism providers (McCool, 2002; Tonge & Moore, 2007; Weber, 2007). Therefore, understanding visitor satisfaction becomes important to PA managers, as a way not only to validate experiences (Hornback & Eagles, 1999) and justify expenses (Weber, 2007) but also to assist managers in the prudent allocation of limited resources.

Several studies on visitors' satisfaction from nature-based tourism (NBT) have been made widely internationally and limited in Indian context. Most of which reflect the uncertainty in selecting the determinant variables for measuring visitors' satisfaction from NBT. Past literature, on the one hand, concentrates on describing satisfaction by the evaluation consumers make of perceived quality from their expectations, while the more recent trends perceive emotions consumers experience as the determinant factors in creating satisfaction (De Rojas & Camarero, 2008). Recent studies, however, reflect the importance of attributes like accommodation facility and hospitality offered (Nam, 2011; Regmi & Walter, 2016; Sati, 2018) entry fee (Badola et al., 2018), visitors safety

(Gstaettner, Kobryn, Rodger, Phillips, & Lee, 2018; Monz, Cole, Leung, & Marion, 2009), environmental conservation (Shi et al., 2018), interpretations (Kim & Coghlan, 2018; Moscardo & Hughes, 2018), and social involvement (Ramkissoon, Mavondo, & Uysal, 2018)) as critical in determining the overall satisfaction of consumers (visitors) from NBT.

Evaluating visitor satisfaction

Although the value of focusing on a generic measure of "overall satisfaction" has been questioned in the literature (Manning, 1999), and there is increasing focus on more specific benefits and learning impacts as key outcomes (Ballantyne, Packer, & Falk, 2011; Roggenbuck & Driver, 2000), wherein visitor satisfaction remains a key output that interests managers. One common method used to investigate satisfaction is importance–performance analysis (IPA). IPA was introduced by Martilla and James (1977), which is based on the mean importance and performance scores obtained by respondents for specific attributes related to a product. In this study, ecotourism experience was focused and therefore IPA was used to examine the importance and performance of service quality attributes and the desire and attainment of specific benefits. Another related approach evaluates performance–importance gap (performance minus importance) scores as a measure of satisfaction (Taplin, 2012). Wherein, a negative gap score indicates importance or desire was higher than attainment and hence management attention to this attribute is needed more. Whereas, a positive gap score indicates performance or attainment exceeds desire or importance and can be used to identify areas not requiring additional resources. Traditional IPA uses rectangular quadrants of the performance versus importance plot to determine management action, whereas gap analysis uses triangular regions as performance minus importance gaps equal to a specific value (such as zero) correspond to diagonal lines on the IPA plot. IPA is a commonly used method of analysis in tourism-related research because of its ease of application and ability to be understood by managers and applied to the development of strategic recommendations (Deng, 2007; Oh, 2001; Tonge & Moore, 2007).

Determining visitors' satisfaction towards the entire experience becomes of paramount importance for the success of any ecotourism destination (Drumm & Moore, 2005). IPA has been successfully employed to understand customer satisfaction and prioritize service quality improvements (Bacon, 2003) in a wide range of contexts, including in the evaluation of park facilities (Hollenshorst, Olson, & Fortney, 1992; Mengak, Dottavio, & O'Leary, 1986; Wade & Eagles, 2003), wildlife parks (Akama & Kieti, 2003; Taplin, 2012), outdoor recreation sites (Tarrant & Smith, 2002), ski resorts (Hudson & Shephard, 1998; Uysal, Howard, & Jamrozy, 1991), and hot springs tourism (Deng, 2007). IPA is based on the assumption that satisfaction is affected by both the importance of an attribute and perceived performance of that attribute. IPA matrices (Figure 1) graphically illustrate the disparity between the importance and satisfaction of individual attributes in a way that is easy to understand and interpret (Duke & Persia, 1996). The scores of importance and performance are plotted on an IPA matrix, which is divided into four quadrants. The quadrants are labeled "possible overkill," "keep up the good work," "low priority" and "concentrate efforts here," prescribing prioritization of attributes for

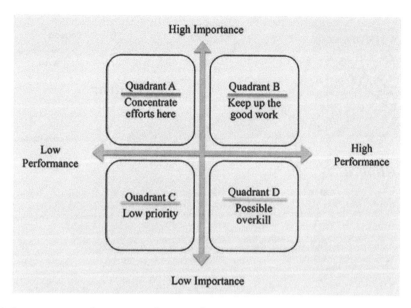

Figure 1. Importance–performance analysis quadrants.

improvement. Attributes in the "concentrate efforts here" quadrant (high impor-tance and low performance) require immediate attention and should be improved for visitor satisfaction. Attributes located in the "keep up the good work" quadrant have both high importance and satisfaction scores and could be used as major strengths in marketing activities. Attributes in the "low priority" quadrant (low importance and low performance) do not significantly affect visitor satisfaction and do not require additional effort. Attributes in the "possible overkill" quadrant (high importance and low performance) indicate that resources committed to these attributes could be better used on other attributes. Based on this analysis, manage-rial actions can be determined for immediate improvement efforts on the attributes in the "concentrate efforts here" quadrant as suggested by Martilla and James (1977).

Thus, the objectives of this study were to (i) identify sanctuary's attributes contribut-ing to overall visitor's satisfaction from the ecotourism experience; (ii) determine key attributes reflecting maximum variance in satisfaction responses using factor analysis, (iii) to assess measure of satisfaction using gap analysis; (iv) to determine significant socio-demographic/trip characteristics variables contributing to overall positive satis-faction using chi-square analysis, and identify attributes where efforts need to be concentrated the most.

Methods

Study area

Binsar Wildlife Sanctuary (BWLS) is located in the Kumaon administrative division of the Uttarakhand State of India (Figure 2). Presently, it comes under the two districts of Uttarakhand, that is, Almora and Bageshwar and is situated at an altitude varying

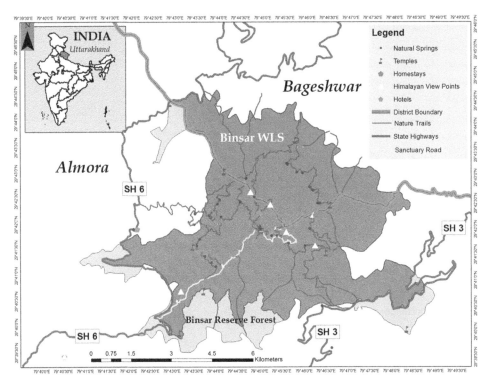

Figure 2. Location map and ecotourism products offered at Binsar Wildlife Sanctuary of Uttarakhand.

between 1400 and 2500 m above sea level. The geographical coordinates of BWLS are 29°39′–29°44′ N latitudes and 79°41′–79°49′ E longitudes. As per the Binsar Management Plan 2015–2016 to 2025–2026, BWLS covers an area of 47.07 km^2. Snowfall in winter varies from 3 to 30 in. Rainfall in Binsar is unpredictable and ranges from 26 to 120 cm. The mean monthly temperature ranges from 0 to 15.5°C during winter and from 17.2 to 26.6°C during summer. The terrain throughout the sanctuary is hilly and is characterized by deep ravines, crevices and elevated ridges. The general landscape is characterized by deeply dissected valleys and steep (30°–45°) slopes. The sanctuary comprises of five hamlets that are not the revenue villages sustaining a total population of 262 residents and 17 accommodations (Bhalla, Coghlan, & Bhattacharya, 2016). The ecotourism products offered at BWLS include enjoying Himalayan views, wildlife sightings, hiking, village-visits, traditional art, culture and cuisine, homestays and historical setups. The sanctuary is open to its visitors throughout the year wherein, domestic tourism supersedes international tourism, as per the tourists records made available at BWLS gate.

Questionnaire design

A self-administered questionnaire was used to measure the perceived importance and performance of various attributes of the sanctuary, resulting in the use of an IPA. A review of previous studies (Ryan & Saward, 2004; Taplin, 2012; Tomas,

Crompton, & Scott, 2003) and consultation with sanctuary officers were used to generate a list of relevant attributes to be included in the survey. Following Oh (2001), an initial list of 20 attributes was reduced to 16, in order to use a high level of abstraction rather than specific attributes, and due to survey length restrictions. The survey then asked how important each specific attribute was to the participant, using a five-point Likert scale, ranging from very unimportant (1) to very important (5). Similarly, the performance scale requested that visitors rate their level of satisfaction with the performance of each attribute on a five-point Likert scale, ranging from perform worst (1) to perform best (5). A space was provided for non-response options, as recommended by Ryan and Garland (1999). The questionnaire also included fields to collect relevant socio-demographic and travel characteristics information including age, education, profession, travel nature and type of visit. Prior to the formal survey, a preliminary trial of the questionnaire involving 25 visitors to the BWLS was conducted to modify any ambiguous or misleading items. The pre-test allowed refinement of the survey format and rewording of certain questions.

Data collection

The formal survey was conducted during peak tourism seasons from April 2014 to March 2015. The peak hours for the sanctuary, from 9 a.m. to 12 p.m. and 2 p.m. to 4 p.m. were chosen for the survey period on each day. Reception at the sanctuary gate and accommodations inside the sanctuary were selected as the sampling locations, based on the rationale that people would be more willing to participate in a survey before entering or while relaxing during their free time. Visitors were selected on random basis for participation in the survey; particularly who showed their interest. Informed consent was obtained before proceeding. Only one adult per group was asked to participate. Out of 200 responses, 51 were excluded due to lack of responses to specific questions. A 74.5% response rate was obtained, resulting in 149 responses for analysis.

Statistical analysis

The data derived from the questionnaire were systematically coded and analyzed using SPSS (Statistical Package for the Social Sciences) software (IBM Corp. 2011). The satisfaction scale was factor analyzed using principal component analysis with varimax rotation to examine internal reliability and validity of the scales. An eigenvalue of 1.00 or more was used to identify potential factors. Factor loadings more than .40 were used to select variables. The arithmetic averages of importance and performance scores were calculated, and paired t-tests were then conducted to seek differences between them. Gap analysis often accompanies IPA quadrant analysis and provides a statistical examination, such as conducting t-tests for non-zero gaps (Taplin, 2012). The gap is defined as the mean performance minus the mean importance. In addition to IPA, significant socio-demographic and trip characteristics variables contributing to overall positive satisfaction were determined using chi-square analysis (at 5% alpha level of significance).

Results

Participants' profile

The sample included 75 (50.3%) females and 74 (49.7%) males among the 149 respondents. The largest age group was that of persons aged below 55 years (88.6%), whereas the smallest was that of persons aged 55 or more. In terms of professional profile, most respondents were students (32.9%), though the rates of private sector workers (31.5%) and government employees/self-employed (16.8%) were relatively high. With regard to trip characteristics, most of the respondents visited BWLS in an unplanned manner (54.4%) and, for a day visit (67.1%) trip. A detailed profile of survey participant characteristics is shown in Table 1.

Factor analysis of attributes

The set of attributes were assembled from a variety of sources, so an exploratory factor analysis was conducted to verify the construct validity and assess the presence of underlying themes within a data set. An examination of the Kaiser–Meyer–Olkin (KMO) measure of sampling adequacy suggested that the sample was factorable (KMO = .633). The p-value of Bartlett's test of sphericity was almost zero. Factor analysis was conducted on the other 16 items of satisfaction in order to have maximum explanation of the total variance by the least common factors. The factor analysis was based on the PCA with varimax rotation, eigenvalue exceeding 1, and factor loadings exceeding .4. Four latent factors were thus extracted. According to Hair, Anderson, Tatham, and Black (1998), when one item reveals a highest factor loading above .45, the item will be allocated in the factor. However, when the item is among different factors and the gap of factor loading is <.1, the gap of the item in different factors is insignificant. The item should thus be eliminated. Thus, in total, three items were eliminated. 13 items were kept, and they were allocated to four factors. After extracting the factors, based on the items with higher factor loading in different factors, this study

Table 1. Demographic and travel characteristics of respondents.

Characteristic	Type	Number	%	Satisfied (%)	Non-satisfied (%)	p-value
Gender	Categorical					
Male		74	49.7	50.0	48.0	.855
Female		75	50.3	50.0	52.0	
Age	Categorical					
<55 years		132	88.6	88.7	88.0	.919
55 years		17	11.4	11.3	12.0	
Profession	Categorical					
Student		49	32.9	34.7	24.0	.366
Government servants		25	16.8	18.5	8.0	
Private sector		47	31.5	29.8	40.0	
Self-employed		25	16.8	15.3	24.0	
Retired		3	2.0	1.6	4.0	
Trip characteristics	Categorical					
Planned		68	45.6	50.0	24.0	.017*
Unplanned		81	54.4	50.0	76.0	
Type of visit	Categorical					
Day visit		100	67.1	63.7	84.0	.049*
Night visit		49	32.9	36.3	16.0	

named the factors as "Hospitality and logistics," "nature and social setup," "amenities" and "ecotourism products." The cumulated variance of the all four factors was found to be 49.53%. The factor analysis result is shown in Table 2.

Reliability and validity of attributes

Regarding reliability test of factors (Table 2), this study examined internal consistency using Cronbach's α. The α value of "hospitality and logistics" was .735, "natural and social setup" was .644. For "amenities" and "ecotourism products," the Cronbach's α value was found to be <.6. Thus of the four factors thus extracted, only two were found to be internally consistent. But, however less internally consistent, the items of these two factors (4 items), and the three eliminated items were also included in the IPA analysis because of its importance in context to ecotourism in PAs. Since α value was approximate to or above .6, the questionnaire revealed a certain degree of reliability (Cuieford, 1965; Nunnally, 1978).

Importance and perceived performance of sanctuary visits

Table 3 contains the mean performance, mean importance, and the gap between them for each attribute, as well as the statistical significance of how the gaps differ from each other. The mean scores of importance ranged from a high of 4.93 to a low of 4.46. Importance was highest for "social space" (mean = 4.93), followed by "visitor safety" (mean = 4.92), "view point conditions" (mean = 4.91), "food quality" (mean = 4.89), and "accommodation facility," "environmental conservation" and "user facilities" (mean = 4.87). The results indicated that "hotel tariff" (mean = 4.46), and "entry fees" (mean = 4.50) were of comparatively lesser importance to sanctuary visitors than other attributes.

In terms of the mean performance, the scores for the all 16 attributes ranged from a high of 4.77 to a low of 2.66. "ease of viewing" (mean = 4.77) was identified as being the attributes on which the sanctuary performed best, followed by "species diversity" (mean = 4.42), "local development" (mean = 4.34), "view point conditions" (mean = 4.26) and "environmental conservation" (mean = 4.17). Lower scores of performance, however, were recorded for "signage and information" (mean = 2.66), "nature guiding" (mean = 2.76), "user facilities" (mean = 3.11), and "food quality" (mean = 3.15), which suggests that the sanctuary may require improvement to enhance visitor satisfaction. A comparison of the mean importance and mean performance of each attribute (Table 3) indicates that the performance values of 15 attributes did not exceed importance values (negative disconfirmation). The only attribute for which performance approximately matched expectation was the "ease of viewing." A series of paired *t*-tests were carried out to verify whether the mean score differences between importance and performance were statistically significant. In 15 attributes, with the exception of "ease of viewing," importance scores were significantly higher than performance scores. This means that the majority of attributes and services provided by sanctuary failed to align with the importance prescribed by sanctuary

Table 2. Factor analysis and reliability test results of experience expectation.

Satisfaction attributes	Principal component factors			
	Hospitality and logistics	Nature and social setup	Amenities	Ecotourism products
(1) Accommodation facility	**.702**	-.328	-.129	-.041
(2) Food quality	**.700**	-.159	.429	-.256
(3) Entry fees	**.646**	-.154	-.154	-.074
(4) Hotel tariff	**.644**	-.191	.009	-.018
(5) Hospitality offered	**.582**	.053	.279	.336
(6) Environmental conservation	.341	**.617**	-.231	-.019
(7) Visitor safety	.403	**.609**	-.139	-.112
(8) Local development	.361	**.558**	-.308	.355
(9) Species diversity	.017	**.518**	-.152	.245
(10) Social space (restaurants)	.310	.233	**.758**	-.159
(11) Signage and information	-.239	.156	**.472**	.352
(12) Trail conditions	.228	-.204	.186	**.635**
(13) View point conditions	.247	-.330	-.233	**.429**
Eigenvalues	2.95	2.01	1.64	1.32
% of variance	18.43	12.57	10.25	8.28
Cumulative %		31	41.26	49.53
Standardized Cronbach's α	.735	.644	.274	.327

Table 3. Results of importance–performance analysis.

Satisfaction attributes	Importance		Performance		Difference (P–I)	t-value	p-value
	Mean	SD	Mean	SD			
Hospitality and logistics							
1. Accommodation facility	4.87	.41	3.34	1.05	−1.54	16.342	.00
2. Food quality	4.89	.31	3.15	1.18	−1.74	16.716	.00
3. Entry fees	4.50	.59	3.48	1.07	−1.02	10.285	.00
4. Hotel tariff	4.46	.78	3.88	1.03	−.58	5.618	.00
5. Hospitality offered	4.80	.48	3.55	.99	−1.25	13.981	.00
Nature and social setup							
6. Environmental conservation	4.87	.33	4.17	.87	−.70	8.974	.00
7. Visitor safety	4.92	.27	3.97	.91	−.95	12.345	.00
8. Local development	4.84	.48	4.34	.81	−.50	6.538	.00
9. Species diversity	4.81	.55	4.42	.91	−.39	5.797	.00
Amenities							
10. Social space	4.93	.25	3.37	1.33	−1.56	14.168	.00
11. Signage and information	4.84	.56	2.66	1.27	−2.17	18.786	.00
Ecotourism products							
12. Trail conditions	4.83	.62	3.63	.99	−1.20	12.196	.00
13. View point conditions	4.91	.37	4.26	.59	−.65	10.818	.00
Interpretations							
14. Ease of viewing	4.79	.50	4.77	.53	−.02	.831	.41
15. Nature guiding	4.66	.78	2.76	.83	−1.90	19.676	.00
16. User facilities	4.87	.35	3.11	.97	−1.77	21.346	.00

visitors; thus, sanctuary visitors were not satisfied with their overall ecotourism experience of the sanctuary. The largest gap between the importance and performance mean scores were seen in the "user facilities," "nature guiding," "signage and information," "food quality" and "accommodation facility" attributes.

Figure 3 presents a comparison of the mean importance and mean performance of the five dimensions (four derived from PCA and remaining one). Performance failed to match importance in each of the five dimensions. A gap between importance and performance levels was highest for "amenities," followed by "accommodation/hospitality" and "interpretations." The only dimension for which performance approximately matched importance was "natural and social setup"

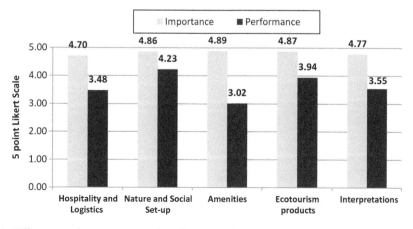

Figure 3. Differences of importance and performance for selected sanctuary attributes.

Importance–performance analysis grid

After obtaining the scores of importance and performance for each attribute, the 16 attributes were plotted on the IPA grid (Figure 4). The plot is split into four areas by plotting two axes derived from the mean of all importance items (mean = 4.82) and the mean of all performance items (mean = 3.64). The matrix in Figure 4 shows that six attributes were identified in the "concentrate efforts here" quadrant, four in the "keep up the good work" quadrant, three in the "low priority" quadrant, and three in the "possible overkill" quadrant. The Quadrant A ("concentrate efforts here") repre-sents items of high importance but low satisfaction, and so the attributes in this quadrant are considered problematic for management and require immediate atten-tion for visitor satisfaction. The six attributes in this quadrant from this study are "accommodation facility," "food quality," "social space," "signage and interpreta-tions," "trail conditions" and "user facilities." Among the 16 attributes, four attri-butes are located in Quadrant B ("keep up the good work"), indicating that these attributes were perceived to be very important to visitors, and at the same time were rated as having a high level of performance. These attributes are "environmental conservation," "safety," "local development" and "view point conditions." Even though all of these attributes appear in the "keep up the good work" quadrant, it was shown that performance scores were rated very high for all except for "safety." The Quadrant C ("low priority") contained attributes with both low importance and performance scores. Three attributes "entry fees," "hospitality offered" and "nature guiding" fell into this quadrant that reflect hospitality and logistics, and interpreta-tions component. Towards which, the sanctuary visitors had low expectations.

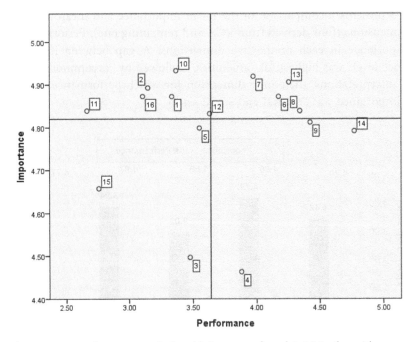

Figure 4. Importance–performance analysis grid. Items numbered 1–16 in the grid are sequentially described in Table 3.

Particular attention should be paid to the fact that performance results even failed to match these low expectations. The bottom right-hand Quadrant D ("possible over-kill") represents high satisfaction and low importance ratings. These items were "hotel tariff," "species diversity" and "ease of viewing."

Chi-square analysis

Chi-square tests examined for frequency differences of responses among demographic and trip characteristic variables of respondents are presented in the Table 1. As shown, gender, age and profession were not found to be significant factors that determine visitors satisfaction from visit to PA in terms of experiencing ecotourism, whereas trip characteristics does. Visitors whose trip were "unplanned" were more likely to be non-satisfied (p-value = .17) as compared to the visitors who had planned visit. In addition, the visitors who took "day visit" to the sanctuary were likely to be non-satisfied (p-value = .49). Thus, the trip characteristics with which a tourist travelled significantly differentiated satisfied visitors from non-satisfied visitors.

Discussion

Visitors' satisfaction in terms of ecotourism experience within a remote mountain destination reflects the interdisciplinary nature of ecotourism studies (Buckley, 2009). Since ecotourism stands on the cornerstones of benefit to environment, benefit to communities, conservation and interpretations (TIES, 2015), all the 16 attributes used in this study reflected these components. However, the factor analysis results accounted for only 49.5% of the variance explained by the 13 attributes falling under the four factors namely hospitality and logistics; natural and cultural setup; amenities and ecotourism products, the remaining three attributes were also considered in the IPA. These three items namely ease of viewing, nature guiding and user facilities, reflect both the intangible and tangible experiences from the interpretations component of ecotourism. BWLS is known for breathtaking view of the Himalayan Ranges, bird-watching and hiking, attracting ecotourists around the globe. These ecotourism products therefore demand nature guides, besides basic user facilities to ensure complete satisfaction of the ecotourists, specifically, which themselves are difficult to identify (Deng & Li, 2015). This paper, therefore, attempted to determine the overall satisfaction of visitors from their visit to a PA primarily known for its ecotourism products, without differentiating visitors as either ecotourists or non-ecotourists.

This research used an IPA to assess the importance and perceived performance of ecotourism experience in the PA of the IHR in order to measure visitor satisfaction levels. The main findings from the research suggest that, the most important attributes identified by BWLS visitors were "social space," "visitor safety," "view point conditions," "food quality," "accommodation facility," "environmental conservation" and "user facilities." On the IPA grid (Figure 4), the attributes categorized into the "hospitality and logistics" dimension appeared to be scattered in all four quadrants. Wherein, none of the attributes in the dimension exceeded 4.0 in the performance score, indicating that continuing efforts are still needed to increase the satisfaction level of visitors in the sanctuary. Whereas, the study area performed relatively well in "nature and social setup" dimension closely aligning with the high expectations of visitors. This supports the fact that sanctuary is working relatively well in terms of maintaining its ecotourism status, which reflects the successful establishment of roots supporting biodiversity conservation (Bookbinder et al., 1998) benefit to local communities (Fennell, 2015) and environment friendliness (Buckley, 2004).

Second, with respect to perceived performance of sanctuary facilities and service attributes, visitors were most satisfied with "ease of viewing," "species diversity," "local development," "view point conditions" and "environmental conservation." This again supports the fact that though less important, the interest of visitors in viewing the Himalayan ranges is well maintained and considered by the sanctuary staff and the accommodation providers, wherein the visitor can have an unrestricted view of The Himalayas. Also, in terms of intangible benefits (Zhang & Lei, 2012) like satisfaction of visitors in terms of sanctuary's environmental conservation and local development efforts, the study reflects positive contribution of the sanctuary in achieving and maintaining its ecotourism objectives (TIES, 2015). However, the interpretations component was still found to be lacking behind, among other crucial pillars of ecotourism. Third, a gap analysis between the importance and satisfaction scores showed that 15 among the 16 attributes had a negative gap, with the performance score of each trending lower than the importance score. This indicates that most sanctuary attributes failed to meet visitors' expectations, resulting in sanctuary visitors having low satisfaction. The least satisfactory attributes included "accommodation facility," "food quality," "social space," "signage and interpretations," "trail conditions" and "user facilities" related to hospitality and logistics, amenities and interpretations factors. Least satisfaction can be attributed to several other factors like nature of the tourist, their intentions, motivations and overall attitudes (Deng & Li, 2015; Johnston, 1998). Thus, in order to determine the overall satisfaction of the visitors, specially attracted towards NBT or ecotourism, needs to be considered in a different manner, separately from general tourists. For this, several researchers suggest different approaches, use of more advanced statistical techniques with IPA and use of non-parametric statistics over other methods (Deng & Li, 2015; Ritchie, Trevor, & Uzabeaga, 2008; Sheng & Chen, 2012; Zhang and Chang, 2016). Subsequently, the study reported to identify the role of trip characteristics of visitors as an important variable in determining their overall satisfaction. Wherein, unplanned day visitors to the sanctuary were likely to be non-satisfied from their visit than planned night stay visitors. Other trip characteristics like purpose of visit and motivation are therefore suggested to include in similar studies in order to determine the nature of relationship between trip characteristics and satisfaction, specifically for ecotourism destinations, where the environment plays an important role. Thus, greater attention should be paid to understand what benefits are desired by the visitors, that directly or indirectly dependent on the environment (biophysical, social, and managerial), through the activities visitors participate in, as suggested by Crilley, Weber and Taplin (2012).

On the other hand, Interpretations' component of ecotourism was found to be in nascent stages within the sanctuary, which needs attention. It suggests that efforts are required to improve the signage and information content within the sanctuary, besides capacity building and trainings of nature guides. This further highlights the role of all concerned ecotourism stakeholders in successful functioning of ecotourism within any destination (Drumm & Moore, 2005). Though willingness of local residents exists in terms of achieving the interpretations component for the sanctuary (Bhalla et al., 2016), yet, it exists as a latent opportunity only. This dimension therefore needs attention in order to not only satisfy visitors in terms of fulfilling their ecotourism experience but also to achieve the overall ecotourism objectives of the sanctuary.

Lastly, as PAs are not only considered a place for recreation but as centers of conservation, education, and research, there exist enormous responsibilities for both, the core decision-makers and the supporting players. Wherein, the pursuit of both conservation and recreation is a dilemma shared by most modern NBT interests (Turley, 1999). In particular, remotely placed PAs are challenged to generate revenue with reduced support and a few numbers of visitors. More and more organizations are thus considering running ecotourism ventures in PA with private ownership to solve these financial problems such as the example of the hometsays program (Bhalla et al., 2016), reflecting efficient public-private partnerships. The results of this study can thus help PA managers and accommodation providers understand visitors' demands as well as their perception of the performance of sanctuary services. The data can also provide a basis for managerial actions to enhance the strengths and improve the weaknesses for better service quality. In regard to analytic methods, this study used IPA in conjunction with a statistical analysis of factor analysis and chi-square to analyze the survey results from multiple perspectives. Other advanced analysis techniques in PA visitor research will help provide greater insight for managerial decision-making, specifically to ensure sustainable practice of ecotourism in ecologically fragile areas.

One of the limitations of this study concerns the generalization of the results, as this research was undertaken during a defined time period at sanctuary in IHR and provided an estimate of visitor satisfaction. Even though the specifics of these results may not be generalized across a wide range of sanctuary, these data can supplement information on the nature of sanctuary visitors and their demands as well as managerial considerations to enhance visitors' satisfaction. Another limitation of this study is that it did not deal with cultural factors. As such, further studies are needed to compare levels of satisfaction across cultures and to investigate the determinants of these differences in satisfaction. Further, incorporation of several attributes in similar studies is subjected to further research and understating. Given the lack of research regarding satisfaction levels of sanctuary visitors, particularly in Asian countries, this study could help PA managers understand the needs of visitors and provide insights into sanctuary management. Whereas, similar research into the visitors' satisfaction addressing different components of ecotourism in similar PA could provide a source of comparison and in depth understanding of ecotourism functioning.

Conclusion

The study identified 16 sanctuary attributes that contribute to visitor's satisfaction from the ecotourism experience for BWLS. Wherein, only 13 key attributes reflected the maximum variance in satisfaction responses using factor analysis. Whereas, a negative gap score for 15 attributes indicated that importance was higher than attainment and hence management attention to these attributes is deemed necessary to improve visitor's satisfaction from ecotourism practice in context of BWLS. Further, trip characteristics were found to contribute significantly to overall positive satisfaction from ecotourism experience in BWLS than socio-demographic variables. The study also prescribes the prioritization of attributes namely user facilities, nature guiding, signage and information, food quality, and accommodation facility for improvement by the service providers managing ecotourism functioning within BWLS.

The study subsequently concluded that the interests and expectations of PA visitors are focused equally on hospitality and logistics and, natural setup. Thus, both need to be prioritized equally and improvements made time to time. PAs need to continue their role as a place for recreation and family outings by providing a safe and convenient environment to view wildlife. At the same time, more managerial attention by key ecotourism players is required to provide diverse educational programs which act as important determinants of overall satisfaction of PA visits. The recent increase of public interest in NBT and the role of PAs as educational and conservation centers are expected to encourage more studies on the demands of PA visitors and their satisfaction with ecotourism experience.

Acknowledgments

The researcher duly acknowledges the reviewers for their insightful comments, the parent University for the Financial Assistance and the Dean USEM. The authors are grateful to the Regional Forest Department of Almora, Uttarakhand, India for providing logistic support and field assistance; the respondent visitors and the villagers for their cooperation; and Indira Gandhi Conservation and Monitoring Centre (IGCMC) of WWF-India for GIS guidance.

Disclosure statement

No potential conflict of interest was reported by the authors.

Funding

This work was supported by the parent University, Guru Gobind Singh Indraprastha University under the Indraprastha Research Fellowship (Award letter number GGSIPU/IPRF/2012/85).

ORCID

Prodyut Bhattacharya (iD) http://orcid.org/0000-0002-4294-5585

References

Akama, J. S., & Kieti, D. M. (2003). Measuring tourist satisfaction with Kenya's wildlife safari: A case study of Tsavo West National Park. *Tourism Management*, 24(1), 73–81.

Bacon, D. R. (2003). A comparison of approaches to importance-performance analysis. *International Journal of Market Research*, 45(1), 55–71.

Badola, R., Hussain, S. A., Dobriyal, P., Manral, U., Barthwal, S., Rastogi, A., & Gill, A. K. (2018). Institutional arrangements for managing tourism in the Indian Himalayan protected areas. *Tourism Management*, 66, 1–12.

Ballantyne, R., Packer, J., & Falk, J. (2011). Visitors' learning for environmental sustainability: Testing short- and long-term impacts of wildlife tourism experience using structural equation modelling. *Tourism Management, 32*, 1243–1252.

Bhalla, P., Coghlan, A., & Bhattacharya, P. (2016). Homestays' contribution to community-based ecotourism in the Himalayan Region of India. *Tourism Recreation Research, 41*(2), 213–228.

Bookbinder, M. P., Dinerstein, E., Rijal, A., Cauley, H., & Rajouria, A. (1998). Ecotourism's support of biodiversity conservation. *Conservation Biology, 12*(6), 1399–1404.

Buckley, R. C. (2004). *Environmental impacts of ecotourism* (p. 389). Wallingford: CABI Publishing.

Buckley, R. C. (2009). *Ecotourism: Principles and practices* (pp. 368). Wallingford: CABI Publishing.

Butler, R. (1980). The concept of a tourist area cycle of evolution: Implications for management of resources. *The Canadian Geographer, 14*(1), 5–12.

Crilley, G., Weber, D., & Taplin, R. (2012). Predicting visitor satisfaction in parks: Comparing the value of personal benefit attainment and service levels in kakadu national park, Australia. *Visitor Studies, 15*(2), 217–237. doi:10.1080/10645578.2012.715038

Cuieford, J. P. (1965). Fundamental statistics in psychology and education (4th ed.). New York, NY: McGraw Hill.

De Rojas, C., & Camarero, C. (2008). Visitors' experience, mood and satisfaction in a heritage context: Evidence from an interpretation centre. *Tourism Management, 29*(3), 525–537.

Deng, J., & Li, J. (2015). Self-identification of ecotourists. *Journal of Sustainable Tourism, 23* (2), 255–279.

Deng, W. (2007). Using a revised importance-performance analysis approach: The case of Taiwanese hot springs tourism. *Tourism Management, 28*, 1274–1284.

Drumm, A., & Moore, A. (2005). *Ecotourism development – A manual for conservation planners and managers: An introduction to ecotourism planning* (Vol. 1, 2nd ed.). Arlington, VA: The Nature Conservancy.

Duke, C. R., & Persia, M. A. (1996). Performance-importance analysis of escorted tour evaluations. *Journal of Travel & Tourism Marketing, 5*(3), 207–223.

Fennell, D. A. (2015). *Ecotourism* (4th ed.). New York, NY: Routledge.

Gstaettner, A. M., Kobryn, H. T., Rodger, K., Phillips, M., & Lee, D. (2018). Monitoring visitor injury in protected areas – Analysis of incident reporting in two Western Australian parks. *Journal of Outdoor Recreation and Tourism.* doi:10.1016/j.jort.2018.04.002

Hair, J. F., Jr., Anderson, R. E., Tatham, R. L., & Black, W. C. (1998). *Multivariate data analysis* (pp. 720). New York, NY: Macmillan Publishing.

Hausmann, A., Toivonen, T., Slotow, R., Tenkanen, H., Moilanen, A., Heikinheimo, V., & Minin, E-Di. (2018). Media data can be used to understand tourists' preferences for nature-based experiences in protected areas. *Conservation Letters, 11*(1), 1–10.

Hollenshorst, S., Olson, D., & Fortney, R. (1992). Use of Importance-performance analysis to evaluate state park cabins: The case of the West Virginia state park system. *Journal of Park and Recreation Administration, 10*(1), 1–11.

Hornback, K., & Eagles, P. (1999). Visitor studies. In K. Hornback & P. Eagles (Eds.), *Guidelines for public use measurement and reporting at parks and protected areas* (pp. 44–54). Gland: IUCN.

Hudson, S., & Shephard, G. W. H. (1998). Measuring service quality at tourist destinations: An application of importance-performance analysis to an alpine ski resort. *Journal of Travel & Tourism Marketing, 7*(3), 61–77.

IBM Corp. (2011). *IBM SPSS statistics for Windows, Version 20.0.* Released. Atmonk, NY: Author.

Johnston, R. J. (1998). Exogenous factors and visitor behavior: A regression analysis of exhibit viewing time. *Environment and Behavior, 30*(3), 322–347.

Kim, A. K., & Coghlan, A. (2018). Promoting site-specific versus general proenvironmental behavioral intentions: The role of interpretation. *Tourism Analysis, 23*(1), 77–91(15).

Lindberg, K., Kreg, M., Stephen, S. F., & Stankey, G. (1997). Rethinking carrying capacity. *Annals of Tourism Research, 24*(2), 461–465.

Manning, R. (1999). *Studies in outdoor recreation. Search and research for satisfaction.* Corvallis: Oregon State University.

Martilla, J., & James, J. (1977). Importance-performance analysis. *Journal of Marketing, 41*(1), 77–79.

McCool, S. (2002). *Tourism in protected area: Continuing challenges and emerging issues for sustaining visitor experiences.* Paper presented at the Celebrating Mountains Conference, Jindabyne, NSW, Australia.

McCool, S. F., & Lime, D. W. (2000). Tourism carrying capacity: Tempting fantasy or useful reality? *Journal of Sustainable Tourism, 9*(5), 372–388.

Mengak, K. K., Dottavio, F. D., & O'Leary, J. T. (1986). Use of importance-performance analysis to evaluate a visitor center. *Journal of Interpretation, 11*, 1–13.

Monz, C. A., Cole, D. N., Leung, Y.-F., & Marion, J. L. (2009). Sustaining visitor use in protected areas: Future opportunities in recreation ecology research based on the USA experience. *Environmental Management.* doi:10.1007/s00267-009-9406-5

Moscardo, G., & Hughes, K. (2018). All aboard! Strategies for engaging guests in corporate responsibility programmes. *Journal of Sustainable Tourism.* doi:10.1080/09669582.2018.1428333

Nam, J. (2011). Brand equity, brand loyality and consumer satisfaction. *Annals of Tourism Research, 38*(3), 1009–1030.

Newsome, D., Rodger, K., Pearce, J., & Chan, K. L. J. (2017). Visitor satisfaction with a key wildlife tourism destination within the context of a damaged landscape. *Current Issues in Tourism, 22*(6), 729–746.

Nunnally, J. C. (1978). *Psychometric theory* (2nd ed.). New York, NY: MacGraw-Hill.

Oh, H. (2001). Revisiting importance-performance analysis. *Tourism Management, 22*, 617–627.

Ramkissoon, H., Mavondo, F., & Uysal, M. (2018). Social involvement and park citizenship as moderators for quality-of-life in a national park. *Journal of Sustainable Tourism, 26*(3), 341–361.

Rastogi, A., Badola, R., Hussain, S. A., & Hickey, G. M. (2010). Assessing the utility of stakeholder analysis to protected areas management: The case of Corbett National Park, India. *Biological Conservation, 143*, 2956–2964.

Regmi, K. D., & Walter, P. G. (2016). Conceptualising host learning in community-based ecotourism homestays. *Journal of Ecotourism.* doi:10.1080/14724049.2015.1118108

Ritchie, B., Trevor, M., & Uzabeaga, S. (2008). *Visitor attraction satisfaction benchmarking project.* Gold Coast, Queensland: Sustainable Tourism Cooperative Research Centre. Retrieved from http://www.crctourism.com.au/wms/upload/resources/90069Richie_AttSatbenchmarking%20WEB.pdf

Roggenbuck, J., & Driver, B. (2000). Benefits of nonfacilitated uses of wilderness. *Wilderness Science in a Time of Change Conference.* USDA Forest Service RMRS-P-15- (Vol. 3). Fort Collins, CO: Rocky Mountain Research Station.

Rome, A. (1999). *Tourism impact monitoring, a review of methodologies and recommendations for developing monitoring programs in Latin America* (pp. 54). Arlington, VA: The Nature Conservancy.

Ryan, C., & Garland, R. (1999). The use of a specific non-response option on Likert type scales. *Tourism Management, 20*(1), 107–114.

Ryan, C., & Saward, J. (2004). The zoo as ecotourism attraction- visitor reactions, perceptions and management implications: The case of Hamilton Zoo, New Zealand. *Journal of Sustainable Tourism, 12*(3), 245–266.

Sati, V. P. (2018). Carrying capacity analysis and destination development: A case study of Gangotri tourists/pilgrims' circuit in the Himalaya. *Asia Pacific Journal of Tourism Research, 23*(3), 312–322.

Sheng, C.-W., & Chen, M.-C. (2012). A study of experience expectations of museum visitors. *Tourism Management, 33*, 53–60.

Shi, F., Weaver, D., Zhaod, Y., Huang, M.-F., Tang, C., & Liu, Y. (2018). Toward an ecological civilization: Mass comprehensive ecotourism indications among domestic visitors to a Chinese wetland protected area. *Tourism Management, 70*, 59–68.

Spenceley, A. (2008). *Responsible tourism: Critical issues for conservation and development* (p. 432). London: Earthscan.

Taplin, R. (2012). Competitive importance-performance analysis of an Australian wildlife park. *Tourism Management, 33*(1), 29–37.

Tarrant, M. A., & Smith, E. K. (2002). The use of a modified importance-performance framework to examine visitor satisfaction with attributes of outdoor recreation settings. *Managing Leisure, 7*(2), 69–82.

TIES. (2015). *What is ecotourism. The International Ecotourism Society Website.* Retrieved from https://www.ecotourism.org/what-is-ecotourism

Tomas, S. R., Crompton, J. L., & Scott, D. (2003). Assessing service quality and benefits sought among zoological park visitors. *Journal of Park and Recreation Administration, 21*(2), 105–124.

Tonge, J., & Moore, S. (2007). Importance-satisfaction analysis for marine-park hinterlands: A Western Australian case study. *Tourism Management, 28*, 768–776.

Treweek, J. (1999). *Ecological impact assessment.* Oxford: Blackwell Science.

Turley, S. K. (1999). Conservation and tourism in the traditional UK zoo. *The Journal of Tourism Studies, 10*(2), 2–13.

Uysal, M., Howard, G., & Jamrozy, U. (1991). An application of importance-performance analysis to a ski resort: A case study in North Carolina. *Visions in Leisure and Business, 10*(1), 16–25.

Wade, D. J., & Eagles, P. (2003). The use of importance-performance analysis and market segmentation for tourism management in parks and protected areas: An application to Tanzania's National Parks. *Journal of Ecotourism, 2*(3), 196–212.

Weber, D. (2007). *Personal benefits and place attachment of visitors to four metropolitan and regional protected areas in Australia* (Unpublished doctoral thesis). University of Queensland, St. Lucia, Australia.

Zhang, H., & Lei, S. L. (2012). A structural model of residents' intention to participate in ecotourism: The case of a wetland community. *Tourism Management, 33*, 916–925.

Zhang, S., & Chan, C.-S. (2016). Nature-based tourism development in Hong Kong: Importance–Performance perceptions of local residents and tourists. *Tourism Management Perspectives, 20*, 38–46.

How user-generated judgments of hotel attributes indicate guest satisfaction

Sangeetha Gunasekar (iD) and Sooriya Sudhakar (iD)

ABSTRACT

User-generated content is a major source of information particularly in tourism industry where consumers seek unbiased and unregulated information. While making their hotel booking decisions, consumers refer to the previous guests' experiences expressed in the hotel reviews across social media. Studies in the literature have focused on enhancing the understanding of what makes customers satisfied or dissatisfied. They have analyzed the text reviews and the patterns in the overall rating and ranking of the hotels given by hotel guests. While most emerging destinations have been studied in the literature, studies related to India, a fast-growing leisure destination are scant. The present study tries to understand the hotel attributes that contribute towards customer satisfaction or dissatisfaction using online reviews for all hotels of Andaman & Nicobar Islands in India. Among the eight attributes identified from the most frequently used words in the text reviews, the study finds that while the location has a significant probability of increasing the ratings of both high- and low-rated reviews, rooms seem to have the most significant impact on lowering the probability of high scores irrespective of positive or negative sentiment review. The study also finds that guests of luxury hotels rate the hotels significantly higher than the guests of midrange and budget hotels.

酒店属性是否会影响顾客满意度: 针对在线评论进行情感分析

简介

如今, 普遍认为用户生成内容是信息的主要来源。这与顾客所需要的无偏不管制信息的行业的关联更为密切, 如旅游业。旅客认为酒店在线文字评论是一种可靠的信息来源, 也是一种可信赖的消息来源。这几个文献研究项目旨在通过分析文字评论, 帮助了解顾客在酒店的体验。

本研究项目的目的是, 将源于新兴经济体印度的经验增添到此篇不断发展进步的文献中。鉴于印度的旅游业发展情况, 考虑到有关此地区的文献研究相对较少, 研究时间间隔较长, 我们的研究项目通过尝试确定哪些酒店便利设施会影响顾客的评论情绪,补充了欠缺的文献内容。据此, 本研究选取了以水上运动和生态旅游而闻名的安达曼群岛和尼科巴群岛（以下简称: A&N）。

数据和变量

本研究基于源于R的开放源代码编程语言——rvest包和stringer包, 开发出一个网页采集程序, 用于从时下最流行的酒店顾客评论独立网站TripAdvisor.in获取来自A&N两地56家酒店的用户生成评论。首先共识别出30663个单词。其次从中删除与酒店便利设施无关的单词（例如, also（也）、can（可以）、just（只是）、get（得到）、amazing（神奇）、experience（体验）等等）。然后根据剩余的单词与其出现的频率进行绘图, 以确定需要分析的相关单词个数。本研究选取了1765个出现频率超过50次的单词进行研究。两位笔者通过进一步手动编码, 生成八个酒店属性: 食品、酒店员工服务、地理位置、酒店设施、客房体验、安全性、服务、物有所值及清洁度。为了确定哪些顾客对酒店提供的服务表示满意, 我们利用stringr包对评论的两极性进行情绪分析。根据积极、消极和零分的极性得分, 确定评论极性。在共计10716份评论中, 有9461份被确定是积极评论, 663份被确定为消极评论, 其余592份被确定是中立评论。在本研究的后续分析过程中, 我们只考虑表示顾客满意的积极评价和表示顾客不满的消极评论。通过对此类评论进行独立分析, 了解哪个酒店属性对酒店整体评分影响最大。就当前分析情况而言, 如果酒店评分为4-5分, 则为高分; 如果评分为3-1分, 则为低分。这种方法旨在对想要打出较高评分的满意顾客与想要给酒店整体打出较低评分的不满意顾客进行区分。因此, 因变量是一个二进制变量, 用1值表示给出积极评论的顾客满意度, 其他用0值表示。

结果

Logistic模型结果表明, 即使酒店拥有优越的地理位置和优质的酒店服务, 有助于获得顾客积极的评论情绪, 但是, 其他便利设施中的客房、安全性、酒店服务、物有所值因素也会影响顾客消极的评论情绪。我们的研究得出了进一步结论, 从酒店类型的角度来看, 与预算型酒店和中档酒店相比, 豪华型酒店顾客的评论情绪更积极。

Introduction

User-generated contents are considered today as a major source of information (Mudambi & Schuff, 2010). This is more pertinent to industries like tourism where consumers need information that is unbiased and unregulated. The online text reviews of hotels are one such source of information that tourists find reliable (Berezina, Bilgihan, Cobanoglu, & Okumus, 2016) and trustworthy (Xiang & Gretzel, 2010). Analyzing these text reviews in helping understand the experience of customers in the hotels has been the primary focus of several studies in the literature (Kim, Bai, Kim, & Chon, 2018).

The objective of this study is to add to this growing literature from the experience of an emerging economy, India. India has been identified as one of the ten fastest growing leisure-travel world tourist destinations in the coming decade by World Travel and Tourism Council report (WTTC, 2017). As per the Travel & Tourism Competitive Index 2017, India is one among the 15 countries that showed the most improvement in the index over the years. Given the growth of India in the tourism industry and that the studies in the literature focusing on this destination are few and widely spaced in time, our study adds to this sparse literature, by attempting to identify the hotel amenities that impact the sentiment of customer's review. In doing so, the study chooses a destination that is known for its water sports and ecotourism, the islands of Andaman & Nicobar. Findings indicate that while the location of the hotel and hotel service improve the positive sentiment of the customer review, rooms, safety, hotel service and value for money among other amenities are seen to impact the negative sentiment of the reviews. Our study further concludes that with regard to hotel types, luxury hotel customers are seen to give a more positive rating as compared to budget and mid-range hotels.

Background literature

In recent years, several studies have focused on better understanding the impact of user-generated contents like online hotel reviews on consumer's decision-making (Cantallops & Salvi, 2014). These user-generated online reviews are found to reduce the information asymmetry in the hotel industry, more so for hotels that are unbranded and lower star rated (Manes & Tchetchik, 2018). The popularity and importance of these online reviews are largely due to the unbiased information that the customers can get from these hotel reviews, particularly with regard to qualitative aspects of the hotel (Xiang & Gretzel, 2010). Further, the user-generated reviews from reputed websites like TripAdvisor.com are seen as unbiased and more trustworthy by consumers (Bernoff & Li, 2008; Xiang & Gretzel, 2010; Chen & Xie, 2008; Sparks & Browning, 2011). These online reviews are also considered a medium for hotels' online reputation building and reputation management, where the managers have started to recognize the importance of utilizing the available online customer reviews to better understand and manage their hotel reputation (Baka, 2016; Berezina et al., 2016).

Thus with the increasing reliance on online reviews in hotel industry both by consumers to make their decisions and hotel managers to build their organizations' reputation, it is necessary to focus on analyzing these big data footprints in more depth. Our study utilizes the text reviews generated for hotels on the website of TripAdvisor to understand the factors that influence the satisfaction and dissatisfaction of consumers in hotels. Several studies in the literature have analyzed the customer satisfaction (rating/ranking) of hotels and factors that influence these ratings and ranking. Among the factors that were studied by Jang, Liu, Kang, and Yang (2018), staff, room and services are seen to significantly impact the overall rating of the hotels. The study included the impact of 30 hotel attributes across 175,268 reviews from 149 hotels in Chicago from 2011 to 2016. While service and staff seemed to have a positive impact on the overall rating, rooms seem to have a negative impact. Kim and Perdue (2013) grouped the hotel attributes into cognitive, affective and sensory grouping and found using an experimental design that consumers in choosing a hotel consider all the three attributes of the hotel. Further among the sensory attributes, room quality was the most necessary requirement.

Schuckert, Liu, and Law (2015), using over 88,000 online reviews from TripAdvisor for Hong Kong hotels, including both English and non-English reviews across star hotels (2 star to 5 star hotels), find that while non-English-speaking hotel guests prefer low-class hotels and find these hotels to be meeting their expectations better (higher satisfaction), English-speaking guests seem to prefer the hotels that are higher end, with overall satisfaction showing a similar trend. Further, with regard to hotel amenities like value, location, sleep, room, cleanliness and service, the study finds varying importance given by English- and non-English-speaking guests to these attributes. A study on similar lines conducted by Liu, Teichert, Rossi, Li, and Hu (2017) included over four hundred thousand online reviews across 8 different languages such as English, German, French, Italian, Portuguese, Spanish, Japanese and Russia generated for over ten thousand Chinese hotels in TripAdvisor. The study attempted to understand the varying preferences of different language speakers on hotel attributes like rooms, location, cleanliness, service and value along with the overall ratings of the hotel. Study finds that while tourists from abroad are seen to lay higher emphasis on services followed by room, value, cleanliness and location, in that order, Chinese-speaking customers were seen to emphasize more on the hotel room with very little emphasis on service.

The overall ratings reflect the customer's satisfaction with the hotel experience. In other words, if the customer's expectations are fulfilled, he or she would rate the hotel higher and if the perceived satisfaction is less than the expectation, this would be reflected in lower ratings for the hotel (Kim, Kim, & Heo, 2016).

However, the distribution of customer's ratings of hotels is seen to be skewed toward higher ratings. As pointed out by Mariani and Borghi (2018), the overall distribution of over 1.2 million hotel customer ratings in London showed a significant leftward skewness. This was further found to be higher for hotels that were classified as high class as compared to low-class hotels. Others (for e.g. Berezina et al., 2016) argue that textual information in electronic reviews provide stronger measure of customer experience as compared to the overall customer ratings of hotels, thus suggesting that doing a text analysis of reviews would give more insights into the factors leading to satisfaction (or dissatisfaction) of customers with hotels rather than analyzing the overall hotel ratings/rankings.

Thus it is important to include along with hotel rating the text analytics of the user reviews to understand the customer's experience. There are many in the literature like Guo, Barnes, and Jia (2017) who have analyzed the text reviews, their sentiments (positive/negative/neutral) and factors affecting the review sentiments along with analyzing the rating/ranking of hotels by customers. Guo et al. (2017), using over two hundred thousand online reviews for over twenty five thousand hotels located in 16 different countries tried to understand the relative importance of various hotel attributes in overall customer ratings. In their study, they have analyzed both the ratings given by customers to each attribute along with the overall rating in a stepwise linear regression model and identifying important attributes across guests of different types using text mining techniques. They find that room experience and service quality have the highest impact on the overall customer satisfaction. Further, using text mining approach they also attempt to identify the features that are emphasized by each category of hotel guests. The study finds that while homeliness, strong event management capabilities were important to 5-star hotel guests, hotel and resort facilities, food quality and room size and decoration seemed more important to customers of 4 to 4.5 stars. Mid-range hotel guests were seen to be more focused on aspects like car parking, checking in and out, hotel staff service and bathroom facilities. Also with regard to pricing, male customers were found to be more sensitive to pricing than female customers.

In another similar study using text mining approach, Berezina et al. (2016) analyzed the satisfied and dissatisfied customer reviews of hotels across Sarasota, Florida, in understanding what aspects of amenities and services offered by hotels influenced the positive or negative experience of customer with the hotel. With over 2510 reviews from TripAdvisor, the study concludes that while the amenities across both sentiments remain same, not providing the service well enough or with delays dissatisfied the customers. Further, tangibles and financial issues seemed to impact the customers who did not recommend the hotels more than those that recommended the hotels to others.

Xu, Wang, Li, and Haghighi (2017), using text mining methodology, study the specific hotel attributes that impact the positivity and negativity of online reviews. Using over 3500 reviews collected for hotels across 100 largest cities in the US, the study finds that positive experience of customers with staff, room, location and value lead to a positive review of the hotel. Further, the study also finds that while star status of hotels impacts all attributes of hotel products and services for both satisfied and dissatisfied customers, similar significant results were not found for all attributes in terms of editor-recommended hotels and hotel type (chain and individual hotels).

Others in the literature find significant difference in consumer ratings of hotels across different types of hotels. Among these, Banerjee and Chua (2016) in understanding the patterns in hotel ratings across hotel type and traveler's profile include reviews from America, Asia Pacific, Europe, Middle East and Africa. The study finds that while Asia Pacific hotels attracted the highest rating among the chain hotel category, Europe received the highest rating in independent hotels. Rhee and Yang (2015a) in another study compare the importance given to various hotel attributes across guests from 2-star and 4-star hotels. They find value to be relatively important for 4-star hotel guests while location was found to most important for guests of 2-star hotels. Their study was based on four hotels in New York City, US.

Summarizing the results from the literature indicate that customer satisfaction in terms of rating/rankings vary across hotel types and customer profiles. Further substantiating the analysis of these rating or ranking with text mining approach provides more insightful results.

While the above studies cover almost all the growing tourist destinations across the world including countries like the US, Europe (Xiang & Krawczyk, 2016; Marine-Roig & Clavé, 2015) and emerging economies like China (Liu et al., 2017), studies specifically focused on India are sparse (Geetha, Singha, & Sinha, 2017). Given India being identified as one of the fastest growing tourist destinations for leisure-travel spending destinations in the coming years (WTTC, 2017), it is important to understand the key attributes that impact the customer satisfaction in India. The present study attempts to contribute toward this gap in the literature.

Data and methods

Data

User-generated reviews were collected from TripAdvisor, the most popular independent consumer review website for hotels (Fang, Ye, Kucukusta, & Law, 2016). As of 2017, TripAdvisor boasts of over 570 million reviews and opinions covering 7.3 million accommodations, airlines, attractions and restaurants worldwide and is considered home to the world's largest travel community of 455 million average monthly unique visitors.

For the present study, the travel destination of Andaman & Nicobar Islands (hereinafter mentioned as A&N) of India was chosen. A&N comprises of 572 small islands with only about 38 islands being permanently inhabited. User-generated reviews for all 56 hotels in A&N were collected from the start of the first review for the hotels till 18 November 2017. rvest and Stringr packages from R, an open source programming language, was used to develop a web crawling program to scrape the data from TripAdvisor.in. Further, to check the accuracy of our program, a random check was done with five reviews per hotel. Content scraped was found accurate. Among the data that were collected included data on review id, overall customer rating, review date and text review in full. In all, 10,716 reviews of customers across all 56 hotels of A&N were collected. Further, the hotels were classified as budget hotels, mid-range hotels and luxury hotels. The number of hotels in each category and percentage of total reviews are given in Table 1.

Among the hotels included, over 47% of hotels were from the luxury hotel category while budget and mid-range hotels formed about 31% and 22%, respectively. Since A&N islands are predominantly tourist destinations, it is probable that luxury hotels are in greater proportion than the other type of hotels. With regard to reviews, the trend is even more strongly biased towards luxury hotels with over 56% of reviews belonging to guests from this hotel category; while the percentage of reviews contributed by mid-range hotel category was over 40%, it was only 5% from budget hotels. Thus for our analysis, we have combined the hotel categories of budget and mid-range hotels to indicate non-luxury hotels.

Further, in identifying the amenities and services of hotels that impact the customer satisfaction, the code was written using Stringr package to tokenize the review text to identify unique words and their frequencies. Total of 30,663 unique words were identified. Next among these, words not related to hotel amenities (like also, can, just, get, amazing, experience etc.) were removed from these set of words. In the third step, the remaining words were plotted against their frequency to identify the relevant number of words to be included in the analysis. There were 1765 words with frequency more than 50 which were selected for the study. The limiting factor in selecting these 1765 words was that words that are in the tails of the frequency distribution occur seldom in the reviews and hence their impact may be considered negligible enough to not include them in the analysis.

The 1765 words selected thus were manually coded by both co-authors to form eight attributes of the hotels. These include food, hotel staff service, location, hotel facilities, room experience, safety, service, value for money and cleanliness. Each of the eight hotel attributes identified includes several synonyms or related words. The word cloud of these 1765 words is represented in Figure 1. As seen from Figure 1, location (beach) is seen to be the most frequently used word with a frequency of over 12,000 times. One

Table 1. Percentage of hotels included in the study.

Type of hotels	Number of hotels	Percentage in total	Number of reviews	Percentage in total
Budget	17	30.9	510	4.8
Midrange	12	21.8	4263	39.8
Luxury	26	47.3	5943	55.5
Total	55	100	10,716	100

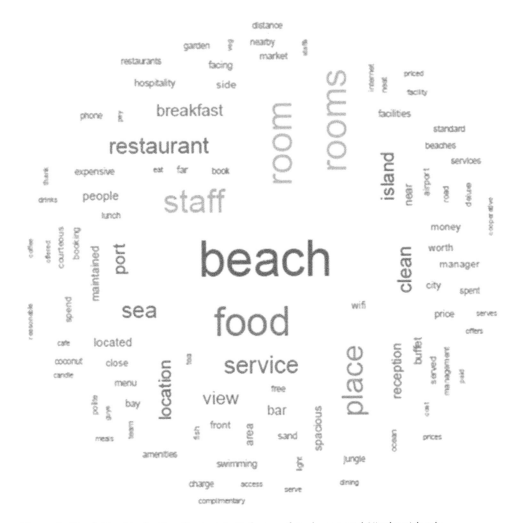

Figure 1. Word Cloud indicating the hotel attributes of Andaman and Nicobar islands.

of the biggest attractions of A&N islands is its beaches. The archipelago of over 300 islands of which only 38 are inhabited provides long stretches of white sand, palm-lined beaches, and most guests visiting A&N islands talk about these in their reviews. Beach is followed by words like food, room/rooms and staff among others being the most frequently used words in the reviews.

Each of the eight hotel attributes were identified, along with the words that were grouped together to analyze the attributes in the reviews. The frequency distribution of words of one such attribute "location of the hotel" is shown in Figure 2.

Customer satisfaction or dissatisfaction: subsamples in the analysis

To identify customers who are satisfied with the services provided by the hotel, we did a sentiment analysis on the polarity of the reviews using stringr package. Based on the polarity scores of positive, negative and zero scores, review polarity was identified. The

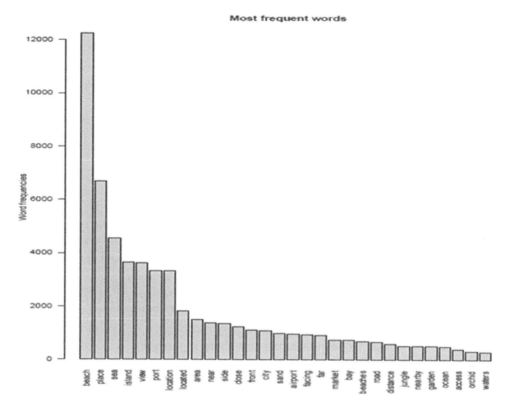

Figure 2. Frequency distribution of words used to describe "location of the hotel" attributes.

polarity scores ranged between −5 and 38 indicating larger scores for positive senti-ments. Of the total 10,716 reviews, 9461 reviews were identified as positive sentiment reviews, 663 reviews were identified as negative reviews and the rest 592 were identified as neutral reviews. Further, for the analysis of this study, we only considered the positive sentiment reviews indicating customer satisfaction and negative sentiment reviews indicating customer's dissatisfaction. These reviews were analyzed indepen-dently to understand the hotel attributes that most contributed to the overall rating of the hotel. Hence, the study includes two empirical models, each for customer satisfac-tion (positive sentiment reviews) and customer dissatisfaction (negative sentiment reviews). Further details of the empirical models are given below in the empirical methodology section.

Overall hotel ratings: dependent variable

The dependent variable is the overall rating of the hotel. TripAdvisor allows the consumers to rate a hotel between 1 indicating "terrible" and 5 indicating "excellent experience" (2 indicates "poor"; 3 indicates "average"; 4 indicates "very good"). Customers who have experienced a positive sentiment would most likely rate the hotel very good (rating of 4) or excellent (rating of 5) depending on the degree of their satisfaction with the hotel. Hence, we combined these two ratings together to indicate "higher ratings" for the hotel. Similarly, ratings 3 to 1, indicating average, poor and terrible, were grouped together to indicate "lower ratings" for the hotel. Table 2 gives the number of reviews that form the two subsamples based on the sentiment of the review. It also provides details of the number of reviews that indicate higher ratings and lower ratings across the two subsamples.

As indicated in Table 2, while the number of reviews are customer satisfaction subsample, there are over 1698 reviews where customers even though have written a positive review have given a lower rating for the hotel. This maybe because customers even though were largely happy with most of the experience, some important aspect of the hotel had given them a negative experience. This negative experience may have led the customer to give a lower score for the hotel.

Further, it is also possible that the ratings of the hotels vary across the type of hotels (luxury hotels versus mid-budget and budget hotels). Similar results were found by others in the literature (Rhee & Yang, 2015b). Table 3 gives details of the number of reviews across the type of hotels and ratings for both sub-samples.

Table 3 indicates that there were higher reviews across mid-budget and budget hotels (6047 reviews) as compared to luxury hotels (4077 reviews). Of these reviews, over 86% of the reviews were rated high across luxury hotels as compared to 73% of hotels across mid-budget and budget hotels indicating that there is a possibility of higher ratings being given by customers who stay at luxury hotels as compared to mid-budget and budget hotels. This is further tested in our study. The empirical model used to analyze this is discussed next.

Empirical models

The present study focuses on understanding the factors that most contribute to the satisfaction or dissatisfaction of hotel customers. Thus in the present study, we estimate two separate regression models each for reviews with positive sentiments indicating satisfied customers and reviews with negative sentiments indicating unsatisfied

Table 2. Number of reviews across the subsamples and ratings.

Subsample	Overall higher ratings (4 and 5)	Overall lower ratings (1,2 and 3)	Total number of reviews
Customer satisfaction	7764	1698	9461
Customer dissatisfaction	116	545	663

Table 3. Number of reviews across type of hotel and sub-samples.

Hotel type	Sub sample	Overall higher ratings (4 and 5)	Overall lower ratings (ratings 1,2 and 3)	Total number of reviews
Luxury hotels	Customer satisfaction	3440	434	4077
	Customer dissatisfaction	48	155	
Mid budget and budget hotels	Customer satisfaction	4324	1263	6047
	Customer dissatisfaction	68	392	
	Total	7880	2244	10,124

customers. The regression models for each of these subsamples of satisfied and unsatisfied customers are given in Equations (1) and (2), respectively.

$$\text{Customer satisfaction} = f(\text{hotel attributes, type of hotel}) + \text{error term} \quad (1)$$

$$\text{Customer dissatisfaction} = f(\text{hotel attributes, type of hotel}) + \text{error term} \quad (2)$$

where the customer satisfaction in Equation (1) is indicated by the overall hotel ratings
given by customers. The ratings range between 5 indicating excellent and 1 indicating
terrible experience of the customer. For the present analysis, the ratings are classified as
high ratings if the ratings were in the range of 4–5 and low ratings if the ratings were in
the range of 3–1. This was done to differentiate the satisfied customers who are
expected to give higher ratings as compared to unsatisfied customers who are expected
to give an overall lower rating for the hotels. The dependent variable is hence a binary
variable indicating customer satisfaction for positive reviews taking the value of 1 and
others taking the value of 0.

To understand the factors that most contributed to the dissatisfaction with customers, Equation (2) is estimated. The dependent variable customer dissatisfaction takes
the value 1 when the hotel guest gives an overall low rating for the hotel a rating that
was either equal to 3 or less than 3. For a higher rating of 4 and 5, the dependent
variable takes the value 0. The sample consists of 663 negative sentiment reviews of
which over 82% of customers gave a rating that was either equal to 3 or less than 3.

As the dependent variables in both regression models are binary variables, logistic
regression analysis was done to estimate the probability of each hotel attribute contributing toward the overall satisfaction or dissatisfaction of the consumer. The results
of the analysis are discussed in the next section.

With regard to hotel attributes, eight hotel attributes are identified for analysis. These
include location, food, facilities, room, safety, service, value for money and cleanliness.
Not all reviewers write reviews including all the attributes of a hotel as shown in Figure 3.
Among the consumers who had a positive experience as indicated by their positive
reviews, while the location was seen to be included in over 95% of the reviews, food
(over 82% of the reviews) and service (over 81% of the reviews) were the next most
frequently included attributes of the hotel. The least included attribute in the positive
reviews was safety with only about 3% inclusion. This is represented in Figure 3.

In the negative reviews, while the lowest attribute to be included is safety with
a similar trend of about 3% reviews including it, the most included attribute is location
and service with over 80% of the reviews including them. Rooms followed by food are
the next most frequently included attributes in the negative reviews.

Thus among the various hotel attributes, location and service are seen to be included
most frequently by both satisfied and dissatisfied customers indicating that these attributes
of the hotel are most important to customers. While the frequently included attribute
indicates their importance to the customer, their significant influence on customers' overall
hotel ratings can be explained only after estimating the logistic regression models, which
would give the odds ratio of an attribute impacting the customer ratings.

With regard to the type of hotel, as indicated in the data section, hotels belonging to
luxury and non-luxury categories of budget and mid-range hotels are included in the
analysis. The dummy variable takes the value 1 when the hotel is a luxury hotel and 0

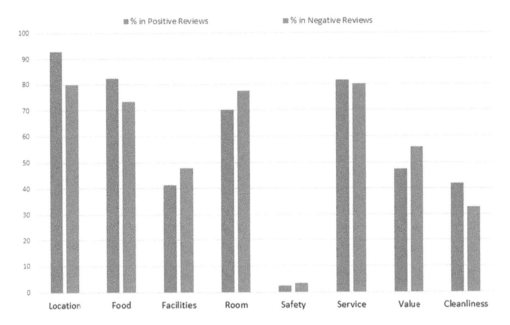

Figure 3. Percentage of reviews that include the hotel attributes.

otherwise. Of the 56 hotels included in the analysis, 12 are luxury hotels while the remaining belong to non-luxury hotel category.

Results and discussion

Analysis to understand the importance of hotel amenities and services in contributing to the customer satisfaction and dissatisfaction is estimated using logistic regression. Estimation results for customer satisfaction given in Equation (1) are given in Table 4. The analysis captures the sentiments of customers who are satisfied with their overall experience with the hotel.

Results indicate that among the attributes that significantly impact the overall customer ratings, location is seen to contribute the most towards higher ratings as seen from odds ratio. Location, particularly the beaches of A&N islands are the biggest attraction in this destination. Most hotels are seen to make the best use of this location advantage to create the eco-friendly environment. This is also reflected in the word cloud depicted in Figure 1, where "beach" is seen as the most frequently used word among all the reviewers of hotels in A&N islands. With regard to attributes that contribute to lowering the overall customers rating of the hotel, the highest contributing attribute is rooms, followed by value for money and lastly facilities. This indicates that customers care more about rooms provided by the hotels as compared to all other attributes. Negative experience related to rooms significantly reduces the overall rating of the hotel even when the customer seems to review the hotel in a positive sentiment. Thus, the managers of the hotels should focus on providing better rooms and room-related amenities which are most important to customer

Table 4. Logistic regression estimation for customer satisfaction.

Variable	Coefficient	Odds ratio
Location	.09***	1.09***
Food	.02	1.02
Hotel facilities	−.04 ***	.96***
Room	−.09 ***	.91***
Safety	.02	1.02
Service	.02	1.02
Value for money	−.07***	.93***
Cleanliness	−.01	.99
Luxury hotel dummy	.1***	1.1***
No. of observations	9461	9461

Note: ***, ** and * indicate significance at 1%, 5% and 10% level of significance, respectively.

Table 5. Logistic regression estimation for customer dissatisfaction.

Variable	Coefficient	Odds ratio
Location	−.10 ***	.90***
Food	−.05	.95
Facilities	.02	1.03
Room	.15 ***	1.2***
Safety	.14 *	1.18 *
Service	.09 **	1.09**
Value for money	.07 **	1.07**
Cleanliness	.05	1.05
Luxury hotel dummy	−.08 **	.92**
No. of observations	663	663

Note: ***, ** and * indicate significance at 1%, 5% and 10% level of significance, respectively.

satisfaction. Further, with regard to the type of hotels, guests of luxury hotels give higher ratings as compared to non-luxury hotels.

Results for negative customer sentiments capturing the customer's dissatisfaction with hotels are given in Table 5.

Results indicate that while hotel attributes like rooms, service, safety and value for money contribute significantly towards lower overall ratings of the hotel, location contributes significantly to higher overall hotel ratings by the customers. Further as seen from the odds ratio, among the attributes that contribute to lower ratings, rooms contribute the most to lower ratings followed by safety, service and value for money attributes. With regard to the type of hotel, guests of luxury hotels are seen to give higher overall hotel ratings even when their overall experience of the hotel has not been up to their expectation. Guests in midrange and budget hotels tend to give lower overall hotel ratings.

Comparing the results for positive sentiment reviews and negative sentiment reviews, location seems to contribute to higher ratings of hotels in both results. Thus the location of the hotel plays the most significant role in increasing the overall hotel ratings irrespective of the customer's experience. As discussed earlier, among the attributes that the customers discussed in the reviews, beach which is included under location was found to be the most frequently used word. The A&N islands are known for their abundant natural beauty with a long stretch of sandy beaches, some of them isolated enough to give tourists the joy of having the beach space to themselves and water sports that come with the location like snorkelling, scuba diving or deep water diving. Tourists also expect to enjoy these when they visit these islands. Having their hotels located either on the beaches or nearby helps them enhance their experience. Similar results are found in the literature where Dolnicar and Otter (2003) find convenience of location to top the attribute list for almost all the studies included in their literature review.

Among the attributes that most contribute to lowering the overall hotel ratings include rooms and value for money. Rooms, if not to the satisfaction of the customers, are seen to significantly increase the probability of customers giving lower overall hotel ratings. Similarly, when hotel guests find themselves being charged higher and not getting their money's worth tend to give lower overall hotel ratings. Our results for rooms are similar to the results found by Jang et al. (2018) where they find rooms to have a significantly negative impact on the overall hotel ratings in Chicago city. The co-occurring words indicate absence of room cleanliness or bad bed condition in the rooms is seen to significantly lower the satisfaction of tourists. Similar importance to hotel accommodation along with fair prices was seen by Chu and Choi (2000) in their study across business and leisure travelers in Hong Kong.

One important feature of the hotel that does not seem to impact the positive reviews but significantly increases the probability of lowering the hotel ratings in negative sentiment reviews is "safety". It is found that guests write about safety when they feel the lack of security in hotels. When the perception of safety is high, the guests either seem to take it for granted or not talk about it much, as seen from the word cloud. The lack of safety seems to significantly impact the negative experience or dissatisfaction for guests. As pointed out by Chan and Lam (2013), safety and security is one of the most important factors that tourists consider when choosing a hotel to stay.

With regard to hotel type, luxury hotel guests tend to give higher ratings both when they are satisfied with their experience with the hotel and when they are unsatisfied. Mid-range and budget hotel guests are more demanding in their expectations and give significantly lower overall hotel ratings if they are dissatisfied. Our results are similar to the results found by Martin-Fuentes (2016) where for a sample of 14,000 hotels in 100 cities across the world they find that higher category hotels to have higher prices and higher scores being awarded by customers.

Conclusion

The impact of user-generated online content on hotel consumers' decision-making has been the focus of several studies in the literature (Kim, et al., 2018). Consumers find the online text reviews of hotels to be unbiased and trustworthy, more so when these reviews are posted on reputed websites like TripAdvisor. While the text reviews for hotels from most emerging tourist destinations have been well documented in the literature, for the fast-growing destinations in emerging economies like India, studies are too few. There is need to understand this growing destination better in terms of what makes customers more satisfied. Among the eight attributes identified for hotels across Andaman and Nicobar islands of India, location is seen to improve the overall tourist ratings of the hotel. Room experience, value for money, service and lack of safety are seen to significantly decrease the overall hotel ratings.

The features identified to have significant impact on customer satisfaction in our study are in line with those that have been of concern to many others in the literature. Convenient location has been identified as one of the top attributes affecting hotel selection and tourist satisfaction (Jang et al., 2018). Hotels' proximity to major attraction in the tourist destination is an important consideration in hotel selection. Thus, hotels investing in their location factor would benefit in attracting larger demand for accommodation (Xang & Krawczyk, 2016). Dolnicar (2002) finds among other attributes location, room, value for money and safety to be included in the top 10 concerns by business travelers in Austria. While good location and value for money is listed among the top priorities expected by business travelers, room experience was seen to be one of the top most factors of disappointment. Our results with regard to negative sentiment reviews indicate similar results for room experience.

Perception of safety by tourists is highlighted in our study by its absence in the positive reviews but having a significant impact on increasing the probability of lowering the overall hotel ratings. Though safety is not the most talked about attribute of a hotel in the reviews, the absence of it creates a high negative impact leading to lowering of the overall hotel ratings. Management of hotels can highlight the safety measures taken by their hotels to attract more guests to their hotels. Also, websites like TripAdvisor can add safety as a feature that could be rated by customers. This would add more value to the review's usefulness.

With regard to hotel type, our results indicate that luxury hotel guests tend to be more satisfied with their stay experience than the budget and mid-budget hotel guests. Similar results with regard to English-speaking guests were found by Schuckert et al. (2015) where they find English-speaking guests to rate their hotel experience at high-class hotels better than non-English speaking guests staying at low-class hotels. Higher start-rated hotels are seen to increase the hotel room bookings (Ye et al., 2009) thus indicating higher satisfaction levels. Studies have also found direct impact of higher customer ratings leading to higher sales of hotel rooms (Öğüt & Onur Taş, 2012). Thus, managers of budget and mid-budget hotels must try and improve their hotel services to influence the experience of their guests, which would then result in higher overall customer ratings and higher room bookings for the hotels.

While positive reviews are seen to improve the revenue for hotels (Phillips et al., 2017), negative reviews are seen to reduce the hotel bookings (Tsao, Hsieh, Shih, & Lin, 2015). Our study identifies some of the important attributes of the hotels that help increase positive sentiment of reviews and impact the negative reviews. Managers of hotels can use this knowledge to understand the tourists' needs and expectations and also identify differently contributing attributes to overall tourist satisfaction. This can further help the mangers improve the facilities provided to tourists.

Limitations and future research

The study has several limitations. While Andaman and Nicobar islands are an important tourist destination in India, there are other more popular destinations across the country. For generalization of results, further analysis is needed with larger text review counts. Also, the study does not distinguish between reviewers from different locations. This might give better insights of differential experiences of hotel stay across Indian tourists and other tourists. For better insights to understanding the positive and negative sentiment of reviews written by tourists, it is important to analyze the polarity of the hotel attribute rather than the polarity of the review. These along with further understanding of review profile could be included in future research.

Acknowledgments

We would like to thank the participants of the conference on "Sustainable Tourism and Hospitality Marketing: An Agenda for Future Research" organized by Department of Tourism and Hotel Management, North- Eastern Hill University (A central university), India, for giving their valuable feedback.

Disclosure statement

No potential conflict of interest was reported by the authors.

ORCID

Sangeetha Gunasekar ⓘD http://orcid.org/0000-0001-7950-3935
Sooriya Sudhakar ⓘD http://orcid.org/0000-0002-9746-7787

References

Baka, V. (2016). The becoming of user-generated reviews: Looking at the past to understand the future of managing reputation in the travel sector. *Tourism Management, 53*, 148–162.

Banerjee, S., & Chua, A. Y. (2016). In search of patterns among travellers' hotel ratings in TripAdvisor. *Tourism Management, 53*, 125–131.

Berezina, K., Bilgihan, A., Cobanoglu, C., & Okumus, F. (2016). Understanding satisfied and dissatisfied hotel customers: Text mining of online hotel reviews. *Journal of Hospitality Marketing & Management, 25*(1), 1–24.

Bernoff, J., & Li, C. (2008). Harnessing the power of the oh-so-social web. *MIT Sloan Management Review, 49*(3), 36.

Cantallops, A. S., & Salvi, F. (2014). New consumer behavior: A review of research on eWOM and hotels. *International Journal of Hospitality Management, 36*, 41–51.

Chan, E. S., & Lam, D. (2013). Hotel safety and security systems: Bridging the gap between managers and guests. *International Journal of Hospitality Management, 32*, 202–216.

Chen, Y., & Xie, J. (2008). Online consumer review: Word-of-mouth as a new element of marketing communication mix. *Management Science, 54*(3), 477–491.

Chu, R. K., & Choi, T. (2000). An importance-performance analysis of hotel selection factors in the Hong Kong hotel industry: A comparison of business and leisure travellers. *Tourism Management, 21*(4), 363–377.

Dolnicar, S. (2002). Business travellers' hotel expectations and disappointments: a different perspective to hotel attribute importance investigation. *Asia Pacific Journal of Tourism Research, 7*(1), 29–357.

Dolnicar, S., & Otter, T. (2003). Which hotel attributes matter? A review of previous and a framework for future research.

Fang, B., Ye, Q., Kucukusta, D., & Law, R. (2016). Analysis of the perceived value of online tourism reviews: Influence of readability and reviewer characteristics. *Tourism Management, 52*, 498–506.

Geetha, M., Singha, P., & Sinha, S. (2017). Relationship between customer sentiment and online customer ratings for hotels – An empirical analysis. *Tourism Management, 61*, 43–54.

Guo, Y., Barnes, S. J., & Jia, Q. (2017). Mining meaning from online ratings and reviews: Tourist satisfaction analysis using latent dirichlet allocation. *Tourism Management, 59*, 467–483.

Jang, S., Liu, T., Kang, J. H., & Yang, H. (2018). Understanding important hotel attributes from the consumer perspective over time. *Australasian Marketing Journal (AMJ) 26*, 23–30.

Kim, B., Kim, S., & Heo, C. Y. (2016). Analysis of satisfiers and dissatisfiers in online hotel reviews on social media. *International Journal of Contemporary Hospitality Management, 28*(9), 1915–1936.

Kim, C. S., Bai, B. H., Kim, P. B., & Chon, K. (2018). Review of reviews: A systematic analysis of review papers in the hospitality and tourism literature. *International Journal of Hospitality Management, 70*, 49–58.

Kim, D., & Perdue, R. R. (2013). The effects of cognitive, affective, and sensory attributes on hotel choice. *International Journal of Hospitality Management, 35*, 246–257.

Liu, Y., Teichert, T., Rossi, M., Li, H., & Hu, F. (2017). Big data for big insights: Investigating language-specific drivers of hotel satisfaction with 412,784 user-generated reviews. *Tourism Management, 59*, 554–563.

Manes, E., & Tchetchik, A. (2018). The role of electronic word of mouth in reducing information asymmetry: An empirical investigation of online hotel booking. *Journal of Business Research, 85*, 185–196.

Mariani, M. M., & Borghi, M. (2018). Effects of the Booking.com rating system: Bringing hotel class into the picture. *Tourism Management, 66*, 47–52.

Marine-Roig, E., & Clavé, S. A. (2015). Tourism analytics with massive user-generated content: A case study of Barcelona. *Journal of Destination Marketing & Management, 4*(3), 162–172.

Martin-Fuentes, E. (2016). Are guests of the same opinion as the hotel star-rate classification system? *Journal of Hospitality and Tourism Management, 29*, 126–134.

Mudambi, S. M., & Schuff, D. (2010). Research note: What makes a helpful online review? A study of customer reviews on Amazon.com. *MIS Quarterly, 34*(1), 185–200.

Öğüt, H., & Onur Taş, B. K. (2012). The influence of internet customer reviews on the online sales and prices in hotel industry. *The Service Industries Journal, 32*(2), 197–214.

Phillips, P., Barnes, S., Zigan, K., & Schegg, R. (2017). Understanding the impact of online reviews on hotel performance: an empirical analysis. *Journal of Travel Research, 56*(2), 235–249.

Rhee, H. T., & Yang, S. B. (2015a). Does hotel attribute importance differ by hotel? Focusing on hotel star-classifications and customers' overall ratings. *Computers in Human Behavior, 50*, 576–587.

Rhee, H. T., & Yang, S. B. (2015b). How does hotel attribute importance vary among different travelers? An exploratory case study based on a conjoint analysis. *Electronic Markets, 25*(3), 211–226.

Schuckert, M., Liu, X., & Law, R. (2015). A segmentation of online reviews by language groups: How English and non-English speakers rate hotels differently. *International Journal of Hospitality Management, 48*, 143–149.

Sparks, B. A., & Browning, V. (2011). The impact of online reviews on hotel booking intentions and perception of trust. *Tourism Management, 32*(6), 1310–1323.

Tsao, W. C., Hsieh, M. T., Shih, L. W., & Lin, T. M. (2015). Compliance with eWOM: The influence of hotel reviews on booking intention from the perspective of consumer conformity. *International Journal of Hospitality Management, 46*, 99–111.

World Travel and Tourism Council (2017), *Travel & Tourism: Economic Impact.* Retrived from https://www.wttc.org/-/media/files/reports/economic-impact-research/regions-2017/world2017.pdf

Xiang, Z., & Gretzel, U. (2010). Role of social media in online travel information search. *Tourism Management, 31*(2), 179–188.

Xiang, Z., & Krawczyk, M. (2016). What Does Hotel Location Mean for the Online Consumer? Text Analytics Using Online Reviews. In A. Inversini & R. Schegg (Eds). *Information and Communication Technologies in Tourism 2016.* Cham: Springer.

Xu, X., Wang, X., Li, Y., & Haghighi, M. (2017). Business intelligence in online customer textual reviews: Understanding consumer perceptions and influential factors. *International Journal of Information Management, 37*(6), 673–683.

Ye, Q., Law, R., & Gu, B. (2009). The impact of online user reviews on hotel room sales. *International Journal of Hospitality Management, 28*(1), 180–182.

Customer brand identification, affective commitment, customer satisfaction, and brand trust as antecedents of customer behavioral intention of loyalty: An empirical study in the hospitality sector

Raouf Ahmad Rather ⓘ, Shehnaz Tehseen, Murtaza Hassan Itoo and Shakir Hussain Parrey

ABSTRACT

The current study presents an integrated model that explores how customer brand identification (CBI), affective commitment, customer satisfaction, and brand trust influence the development of customer behavioral intention of loyalty (CBIL) in the hospitality sector. The underpinning theories of this study are social identity theory and relationship marketing theory. Data were collected in the form of a survey from 345 customers staying at different hotels across six cities in India. The data were analyzed by using confirmatory factor analysis, followed by structural equation modeling. The findings illustrated that the influence of CBI on CBIL is direct as well as mediated by affective commitment, customer satisfaction, and brand trust. The latter three constructs were also direct predictors of CBIL while the influence of customer satisfaction and brand trust on CBIL was found to be mediated by affective commitment as well. These matters have received little attention in marketing generally and hospitality research particularly, and knowledge of the proposed relationships may lead to further research on this topic.

酒店业实证研究: 顾客忠诚行为意向前身—客户品牌识别、情感认同、客户满意度、品牌信任

近些年来, 旅游业和酒店业不断发展, 逐渐成为了全球经济服务业中的主要利润来源。在过去的十年中, 由于固定的客户群能够带来许多益处, 顾客忠诚行为意向 (CBIL) 的概念逐渐引起了学者和专业人士的兴趣。例如: 顾客忠诚度是当今酒店旅游业竞争成功的关键因素, 忠诚客户愿意付出更多, 因而增加收益, 提高钱包份额, 表达更高的购买欲望并且抵制转变。然而, 关于顾客忠诚度的产生因素, 目前尚未达成一致。因此, 本研究使用综合模型, 用以探索在酒店业中, 客户品牌识别 (CBI)、情感认同和品牌信任是如

何影响顾客忠诚行为意向的发展。此项研究依据的理论是社会认同理论和关系营销理论。

数据收集是通过调查的方式进行的，入住印度六个城市的不同酒店的345名顾客参加了调查。选取方法为非概率方便抽样法。数据分析首先经过结构方程模式，然后是验证性因素分析方法。此项发现表明顾客忠诚行为意向受客户品牌识别的直接影响，同时也受情感认同、客户满意度和品牌信任的影响。后三者也是预测顾客忠诚行为意向的直接因素。另外，发现还表明客户满意度和品牌信任对顾客忠诚行为意向的影响程度，也受情感认同的影响。

总而言之，此次实证结果支持了我们的假设。在实证方面，证实了客户品牌识别和客户满意度对于那些想要增加顾客的公司的重要性。就研究本身而言，本研究以采用社会认同理论和关系营销理论的新兴文献为基础，并通过测试和验证所提出的概念模型为其做出了贡献，这个模型是相对于关联替换模型而提出的。因此，在促进顾客忠诚行为意向发展之前，此项研究通过更深入地了解这些社会认同因素和基于营销的关系因素之间的相互关联程度以及它们可能产生的相互作用，进一步扩充了现有知识。此项研究由此拓宽了顾客忠诚行为意向概念和其在酒店业的影响因素研究，广泛促进了服务营销的发展，尤其是有助于当代酒店管理文献的发展。

从管理者角度来看，这一结果也为酒店公司在与顾客建立持久而牢固的关系方面提供了许多启示。因此，本研究就着重维系顾客和发展顾客忠诚度，提出了一些管理建议，这些建议对于(高档)酒店经理和其他利益相关者都是有用的。

最后，现有研究只是在印度这一个国家，并且也只涉及到单一行业（四星和五星的酒店）。因此，以后的研究能够用于预测不同部门、不同行业以及不同国家之间的关系

1. Introduction

Over the years, the tourism and hospitality industry is constantly expanding and has become a leading profit earner in the service sector of the global economy (Liat, Mansori, Chuan, & Imrie, 2017; UNTWO, 2017). Owing to the competitive nature of this industry, every country strives to capture the tourism market by offering better tourism products and/or services. Furthermore, revolutionary changes in this industry such as the emergence of online accommodation booking platforms and low-fare airlines have made traveling more convenient and affordable. Overall, international tourist arrivals are likely to increase globally by 3.3% a year between 2010 and 2030, reaching 1.8 billion by 2030. Between 2010 and 2030, the increase of international tourist arrivals in emerging economies (4.4% a year) is likely to be twice the increase of arrivals in advanced economies (2.2% a year) (UNWTO, 2017). The growth in tourist arrivals in India has spurred the construction of new upscale hotels. This makes India a good platform for studies related to tourists' behavior and the hospitality industry.

As a major player in the tourism industry, the hospitality sector contributes greatly to the success of tourism in a country. The hospitality sector's total contribution to GDP in India stood at US$ 208.9 billion (9.6% of GDP) in 2016 and is forecast to rise by 6.7% in 2017, and to rise by 6.7% per annum to Rs 28,491.8 billion (US$ 424.5 billion), 10% of GDP in 2027 (IBEF, 2018). Hotels in emerging markets, such as India and China, have attracted customer attention in recent years due to increasing disposable incomes and an increase in the number of international events. In fact, these markets are estimated to make up around 10% of the global luxury hotel sector (PRNewswire, 2016). Consequently, India was seen as appropriate countries within which to undertake this study.

For the past decade, the concept of customer behavioral intention of loyalty (CBIL) has received growing interest among academics and professionals as having a loyal customer base leads to numerous benefits (Ali, Ryu, & Hussain, 2016; Huang, Cheng, & Chen, 2017; Martinez & Rodriguez Del Bosque, 2014; So, King, Sparks, & Wang, 2013; Sui & Baloglu, 2003). For example, customer loyalty is the key to success in today's competitive hotel industry (Mattila, 2006; Tanford, 2016). Customer loyalty is a profitable approach since, as a mature industry, the hospitality business must pursue market share gains, rather than market-growth gains (Tanford, 2016). Furthermore, loyal customers are willing to pay more, increase profitability, enhance share of wallet, express higher buying intentions, and resist switching (Kandampully, Zhang, & Bilgihan, 2015).

However, there is still no consensus on the factors that generate customer loyalty (Huang et al., 2017; Martinez & Rodriguez Del Bosque, 2014). Previous studies have examined vital marketing constructs as CBIL antecedents such as customer satisfaction (Martinez & Rodriguez Del Bosque, 2013; Rather & Sharma, 2017), trust (Martinez & Rodriguez Del Bosque, 2014), perceived service quality and perceived value (Han & Hyun, 2017; So et al., 2013), customer engagement (Hollebeek, Srivastava, & Chen, 2016; Rather, 2018; Rather & Sharma, 2017; Sharma & Rather, 2016), and affective commitment (Mattila, 2006; Sui & Baloglu, 2003). Although these findings have shed light on the factors that lead to the development of CBIL from a customer's perspective, few researchers have examined customer brand identification (CBI) development from a social identity perspective (Elbedweihy, Jayawardhena, Elsharnouby, & Elsharnouby, 2016; He, Li, & Harris, 2012; Huang et al., 2017). The development of understanding regarding loyalty's key drivers—while debated—is crucial for contemporary hospitality firms given its direct effect on their competitiveness and profitability (Kandampully et al., 2015; Reichheld & Sasser, 1990). This study therefore responds to Kandampully et al. (2015)'s call for the undertaking of further empirical research exploring the importance of customer loyalty's antecedents in the hospitality sector.

Various researchers believe that the concept of customer/consumer brand identification offers a deeper comprehension of marketing and/or brand management (He et al., 2012; Huang et al., 2017; Martinez & Rodriguez Del Bosque, 2014; Rather & Sharma, 2016a; Stokburger-Sauer, Ratneshwar, & Sen, 2012; Su, Swanson, Chinchanachokchai, Hsu, & Chen, 2016; Tuskej & Podnar, 2018). Despite this, the effects of CBI on development of CBIL remain comparatively unexplored in service marketing, particularly in hospitality (Huang et al., 2017; Rather, 2017; So et al., 2013). Furthermore, the literature on branding typically focuses on CBIL and less on the concept of commitment, both of which are concepts generally studied together in the literature on relationship marketing (Martinez & Rodriguez Del Bosque, 2013; Tanford, 2016; Tuskej, Golob, & Podnar, 2013). The future study therefore could be interesting by testing how consumer's identification and affective commitment influence loyalty and/or purchase behavior (Tuskej et al., 2013). Furthermore, investigation in other countries, particularly developing countries, is also needed to advance the generalizability of results in demonstrating the development process of customer loyalty. As theoretical models employed in one context (i.e. Western context) generally reveal disparities when applied in a different context that has its own unique characteristics, there is a need for further investigation to develop new theories, methodologies, and models (Elbedweihy et al., 2016; Martinez & Rodriguez Del Bosque, 2014).

In response to this gap, we develop a model that integrates social-exchange and social identity-related concepts, which reveals a significant theoretical fit based on their shared social, interactive nature. Consequently, despite their acknowledged significance, the impact of CBI and satisfaction on CBIL remain unexplored within the broader hospitality sector, including the hotel subsector, as investigated in this study (Huang et al., 2017). Furthermore, previous theoretical literature had stressed on the direct influence of CBI on CBIL but failed to consider the effects of mediating variables (He et al., 2012; Tuskej et al., 2013), specifically in the context of hospitality (Martinez & Rodriguez Del Bosque, 2014; So et al., 2013; Su et al., 2016). We construct a unifying framework that allows the simultaneous investigation of these theoretical perspectives that collectively facilitate the development of enhanced understanding of CBIL's underlying relational processes within the hospitality sector (Rather, 2018; So et al., 2013). For instance, hotels are coping with growing customer demand, coupled with severe competition, the emergence of new technologies such as social media, sharing economy, and the growing role of customer interactions to cocreate value, which have raised the importance of adopting customer-centric strategies (Tuskej & Podnar, 2018).

This study provides two main contributions. First, by developing an integrative social identity/relationship marketing-based model, we contribute to the current understanding of the role of key relational concepts, including customer satisfaction, hotel brand trust, affective commitment, and CBIL, thus fitting with relationship marketing's broader scope. To advance this understanding, we develop and test a theoretical model, which is first subjected to confirmatory factor analysis (CFA), followed by structural equation modeling (SEM) analyses by using a sample of 345 hotel customers sourced from Indian four-star and five-star hotels. Second, we provide managerial suggestions centered on customer retention and loyalty development that are expected to be useful to (upscale) hotel managers and other stakeholders (Hollebeek et al., 2016; Rather, 2018).

2. Conceptual framework and hypotheses development

In line with social identity theory (SIT) and relationship marketing theory (RMT), customer brand identification, customer satisfaction, brand trust, and affective commitment are adopted as key antecedents of CBIL in the model (see Figure 1). This study also investigates the consequent antecedents and consequences of customer satisfaction. Therefore, H1, H2, H3, and H4 are supported by *social identity theory*, consistent with (Martinez & Rodriguez Del Bosque, 2013; So et al., 2013; Tuskej & Podnar, 2018). Similarly, H5, H6, H7, H8, and H9 are supported by the *relationship marketing theory* consistent with (Liat et al., 2017; Van Tonder & Petzer, 2018). This section discusses the key research constructs and their hypothesized relationships.

2.1. Social identity theory (SIT)

The social identity theory (SIT) is the primary theoretical foundation of identification in both marketing literature and organizational studies (Lam, Ahearne, Mullins, Hayati, &

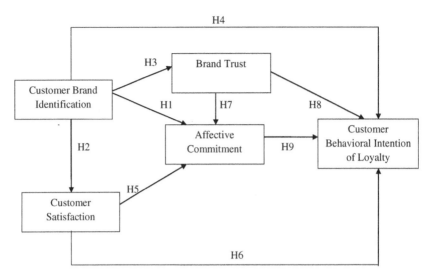

Figure 1. Conceptual model.

Schillewaert, 2013; Tajfel & Turner, 1986). The SIT advocates that people usually go beyond their personal identity to develop a social identity (Bhattacharya & Sen, 2003; Tajfel & Turner, 1986). Based on the SIT, CBI explains why individuals are able to relate to firms (Tajfel & Turner, 1986). Drawing from the SIT and organizational identification, Bhattacharya and Sen (2003) extended the concept of customer identification to customer–brand relationships. Although, in spite of the theory enlightening relationship marketing success for several years (e.g. Bhattacharya & Sen, 2003; Elbedweihy et al., 2016) and likely impacting on process through which consumer experiences unfold (Fujita, Harrigan, & Soutar, 2018), its (SIT) role in marketing and hospitality has been mostly underexplored (Lam et al., 2013; Martinez & Rodriguez Del Bosque, 2013). Customer identification that is essentially a perceptual construct involves identity fit and identity matching (Bhattacharya & Sen, 2003). Individuals likely go outside their self-identity to develop a social identity by classifying themselves and others into various social categories such as organizational membership (Ashforth & Mael, 1989; Bhattacharya & Sen, 2003). Customer identification, underpinned by SIT and self-categorization theory, is when an individual sees himself/herself as psychologically intertwined with the characteristics of a group (So et al., 2013).

2.2. Relationship marketing theory

In an era of global competition and market turbulence, the need for relationship marketing cannot be underestimated. To remain competitive, firms recognize the importance of building and maintaining relationships with their customers. Service firms (e.g. hospitality/hotel firms) can establish relationships with their customers (Morgan & Hunt, 1994; So et al., 2013) and so relationship marketing practices have been extensively studied within the services marketing domain (Brodie, 2017, p. 20). Seminal contributors have defined relationship marketing as "attracting, maintaining, and—in multiservice organizations—enhancing customer relationships" (Berry, 1983,

p. 25) or "attracting, developing, and retaining customer relationships" (Berry & Parasuraman, 1991, p. 133). Berry (1983, p. 236) further suggests that firms practicing relationship marketing should focus on the provision of a core service and must ensure the relationship is customized according to the individual's needs. Additionally, the core service must be enhanced with extra benefits and should be correctly priced to foster customer loyalty. Marketing initiatives must also be directed toward employees to ensure good service is provided to customers. Grönroos (1994, p. 9) believes that relationship marketing practices focus on two parts: attracting customers to the firm, and the subsequent building of relationships with these customers to accomplish the desired economic goals. However, established relationships can only be maintained and enhanced if promises made to customers are kept (Grönroos, 1994, p. 9).

In the relationship marketing domain, relationship quality is considered an important concept that indicates the closeness or intensity of the relationship between a firm and its customers (Vesel & Zabkar, 2010, p. 1336). Although several factors attribute to relationship quality, satisfaction, trust, and affective commitment are regarded as central components or predictors of relationship quality (Van Tonder & Petzer, 2018; Vesel & Zabkar, 2010). Hence, for the purpose of this study, satisfaction, brand trust, and affective commitment are further explored to determine their effect on CBIL.

2.3. Customer brand identification

Researchers examining hospitality and tourism have described CBI as an essential but underutilized construct (Martinez & Rodriguez Del Bosque, 2013; So et al., 2013). As aforementioned, the SIT describes that individuals usually go beyond their personal identity to build a social identity (Bhattacharya & Sen, 2003; Tajfel & Turner, 1986). Customer brand identification is either defined as the extent to which the consumer sees his or her own self-image as overlapping with the brand's image (Bhattacharya & Sen, 2003) or as a customer's psychological state of perceiving, feeling, and valuing his or her belongingness with a brand (Lam et al., 2013). Customers build their sense of self and express themselves through socially identified relationships (e.g. Keh & Xie, 2009).

CBI and how it fits into a framework with other social exchange constructs such as affective commitment provides limited insight so far (Martinez & Rodriguez Del Bosque, 2013; Su et al., 2016). In marketing, researchers expressed that CBI is a crucial variable for developing and building commitment among customers toward a firm (Keh & Xie, 2009). Customers' brand identification is conducive to the development of customer commitment (Tuskej et al., 2013). Through its SIT-informed lens, Su et al. (2016) also establish that higher shared values between hotel service providers and their customers will enhance customer's affective commitment toward having an ongoing relationship with the hotel. We thus hypothesize that CBI is an important driver of affective commitment.

H_1: *CBI has a positive influence on affective commitment.*

Although CBI and customer satisfaction have been recognized as fundamental elements in customer–provider relationships, empirical studies that incorporate both constructs are very limited (Martinez & Rodriguez Del Bosque, 2013; Rather, 2017). Few authors suggested that customers with higher identification levels are more likely to be satisfied with the firm (Bhattacharya & Sen, 2003; He & Li, 2010). In hospitality settings, customers identifying more with (e.g. a hotel) brand will likely to be more satisfied with the hotel through their psychological attachment to the hotel brand (Martinez & Rodriguez Del Bosque, 2013). We therefore hypothesize that CBI is an essential precursor of customer satisfaction.

H_2: *CBI has a positive influence on customer satisfaction.*

Previous researchers in the area of hospitality and tourism did not examine the direct influence of CBI on brand trust, but similar support could be drawn from the relationship between image congruence and brand trust (So et al., 2013). Therefore, the current study suggests that one of the crucial precursors of an identified relationship is brand trust as customers expect to enrich their self-definition and self-esteem through identification with trustworthy brands or organizations (Keh & Xie, 2009). Research indicates that upscale hotel customers who perceive a high congruence of the hotel's image with their own (desired) identity are more likely to have trust in the hotel (So et al., 2013). On the base of this view point, we thereby hypothesize that CBI is a key antecedent to brand trust.

H_3: *CBI has a positive influence on brand trust.*

Research regarding customer brand identification and customer loyalty intention provides limited insight to date (Martinez & Rodriguez Del Bosque, 2013; So et al., 2013). Based on the SIT-informed lens, social identity affects individuals' cognitions, perceptions, evaluations of events, and issues; customers' strong identification with a service brand or offering may lead to increased positive outcomes such as a higher level of customer loyalty (e.g. He et al., 2012; Huang et al., 2017). Hence, customers who identify with a hotel brand are more expected to purchase that brand as a means of self-expression, especially for upscale hotels. We thus hypothesize that CBI is an important driver of customer behavioral loyalty.

H_4: *CBI has a positive influence on CBIL.*

2.4. Affective commitment

Affective commitment to a brand or product has been cited as a vital element to maintain and develop customer loyalty (Curth, Uhrich, & Benkenstein, 2014; Geyskens, Steenkamp, Scheer, & Kumar, 1996; Sui & Baloglu, 2003). In relationship marketing research, affective commitment is an important concept (Curth et al., 2014; Hennig-Thurau, Gwinner, & Gremler, 2002; Rather & Parray, 2018; Sui & Baloglu, 2003). Allen and Meyer (1990) divide commitment into three components—affective commitment, normative commitment, and continuance/calculative commitment. Affective commitment measures the emotional attachment and feelings that customers establish with a firm providing service while continuance/calculative commitment evaluates customers' inclination to remain with the firm, due to a lack of better alternatives. On the other hand, customers who are normatively committed to a firm have a sense of obligation to remain in the relationship (Shukla, Banerjee, & Singh, 2016, p. 324). Affective commitment is a more emotional, or "hotter," factor that develops through personal involvement or reciprocity that a customer has with a firm, resulting in a higher level of trust and commitment (Fullerton, 2003). When customers come to like (or, in some cases, love) a particular firm or brand, they are exhibiting affective attachment or commitment (Fullerton, 2003). As such, this study defines emotional or affective commitment as liking a partner (firm), enjoying the partnership, and having a sense of belongingness (Geyskens et al., 1996; Morgan & Hunt, 1994).

2.5. Customer satisfaction

Customer satisfaction is stated as the psychological state ensuing when the emotion surrounding disconfirmed expectation is coupled with the customer's prior feelings regarding the consumption experience (Oliver, 1997). Customers often make a decision to purchase/repurchase after evaluating whether their experience with the product/service has been satisfactory/pleasurable (Ali et al., 2016; Chen & Chen, 2010). The customer satisfaction model based on the expectation *disconfirmation theory* advocates that customers are satisfied when actual firm performance confirms or outperforms past expectations (e.g. Oliver, 1997). Disconfirmation occurs when there are differences between expectations and outcomes. Negative disconfirmation occurs when product or service performance is worse than expected while positive disconfirmation occurs when product or service performance is better than expected. Confirmation or positive disconfirmation results in customer satisfaction while negative disconfirmation leads to customer dissatisfaction (Oliver, 1997).

The extent to which customers are satisfied with the service may contribute to their future commitment to the service provider. Satisfied customers may become more committed to the service (Hennig-Thurau et al., 2002). Prior research has identified that a customer's evaluation of satisfaction with his/her consumption experience leads to a positive influence on his/her states of commitment (Morgan & Hunt, 1994). High levels of satisfaction have been linked to the development of enduring relationships (Sui & Baloglu, 2003). However, for the purpose of this study, the affective commitment dimension was considered as it has been acknowledged in marketing literature as being strong in establishing consumer behavior (Curth et al., 2014, p. 148). Furthermore, satisfaction is a strong predictor of a customer's intention to revisit a firm (e.g. hotel) and provide positive recommendations and referrals about the firm (e.g. hotel) to others (Su et al., 2016, Rather & Sharma, 2018). In the hospitality sector, customers who are satisfied with the services provided by the hotel are likely to be affectively attached with the services experienced, which in turn would develop customer loyalty toward the hotel (Liat et al., 2017; Tanford, 2016). Therefore, the following hypotheses are proposed:

H_5: *Customer satisfaction has a positive influence on affective commitment.*

H_6: *Customer satisfaction has a positive influence on CBIL.*

2.6. Brand trust

In relationship marketing, researchers regard trust and commitment as constructs that promote efficiency, effectiveness, productivity, and relationship building with firms (Morgan & Hunt, 1994; Sui & Baloglu, 2003). Trust has been defined as the degree of confidence in an exchange partner's integrity and reliability, revealed due to relational qualities such as honesty, credibility, benevolence, and consistency (Morgan & Hunt, 1994). Credibility trust denotes a customer's belief in the ability of the service firm to deliver services of high quality, while benevolence trust is associated with the customer's belief in the firm's ability to offer competent and reliable service (Kandampully et al., 2015, p. 393). Perceptions of trust develop over time and are based on repeated interactions with a service provider (Shukla et al., 2016, p. 325). Alike to satisfaction, brand trust has also been recognized as essential in fostering ongoing relationships with customers in hospitality sector (Martinez & Rodriguez Del Bosque, 2013, 2014).

2.7. Customer behavioral intention of loyalty

Loyalty can be defined and assessed by both attitudinal as well as behavioral measures. The attitudinal measure refers to a specific desire to continue a relationship with a service provider while the behavioral perspective refers to the concept of repeated patronage. Customer loyalty incorporates consumers' revisit/repurchase intention (i.e. behavioral loyalty) and their brand/firm-related perceptions and willingness to recommend the company to salient others (i.e. attitudinal loyalty; Liat et al., 2017; Rather, 2018; Rather & Sharma, 2016b).

Behavioral intention, which is a key aspect of loyalty, refers to "a stated likelihood to engage in a behavior" (Oliver, 1997, p. 28). Customers' intention to repurchase is an essential part of behavioral intention along with word-of-mouth intention (Chen & Chen, 2010; Oliver, 1997). The degree of behavioral intention is reflected in customers' intention to revisit a particular service provider and their willingness to recommend that said service provider to others (Chen & Chen, 2010). Favorable behavioral intentions frequently represent customer's conative loyalty (Chen & Chen, 2010). Researchers have proposed that maintaining loyalty based on relationship marketing has become an essential marketing strategy particularly in hotels (Chen & Chen, 2010; Sui & Baloglu, 2003). To foster customer loyalty, most hotels offer loyalty or reward schemes, routinely track their guests' likes/dislikes, and give deals to repeat customers (Martinez & Rodriguez Del Bosque, 2013), thereby acting as social agents aiming to enhance focal customer interactions and relationships and fitting with our SIT/RMT-informed perspective.

Trust is believed to reduce perceived risk and thereby increase a customer's commitment toward the service provider. Customers are confident that problems will be resolved in time, which subsequently reduces the transaction cost involved (Van Tonder & Petzer, 2018). Previous research acknowledges brand trust as a preceding state for the advancement of affective commitment and a precondition to build valuable relationships with customers (Morgan & Hunt, 1994; Sui & Baloglu, 2003; Van Tonder & Petzer, 2018). Customers with a greater degree of commitment and who have developed enduring relationships with a firm are likely to perceive greater associations between themselves and the firm's offerings/brand (Escalas & Bettman, 2003). In hospitality, affective commitment has been established to be central drivers of loyalty for hotels (Sui & Baloglu, 2003; Tanford, 2016). As such, the following hypotheses are proposed:

H_7: A higher level of brand trust will result in higher affective commitment.

H_8: A higher level of brand trust will result in a higher level of CBIL.

H_9: Higher affective commitment will result in a higher level of CBIL.

2.8. Mediation effects

Few studies conducted in brand management indicated that affective commitment did not mediate the influence of identification on developing positive customer behaviors such as positive word of mouth (Tuskej et al., 2013). Other studies have, however, found evidence demonstrating that the relationship between trust and behavioral intention of loyalty is fully or partially mediated by commitment (Hennig-Thurau et al., 2002; Morgan & Hunt, 1994). In tourism and hospitality, customer–company relationships play a key role in maintaining strong loyalty, especially through satisfaction, emotional commitment, and trust (Tanford, 2016). More recently, researchers examined the influence of CBI on repurchase intention and word-of-mouth communication through the mediating variables of satisfaction and commitment in hospitality literature (Su et al., 2016). Based on above ideas, the following hypothesis is proposed as follows:

H_{10}: Affective commitment, customer satisfaction, and brand trust mediate the relationship between CBI and CBIL.

3. Methodology

3.1. Sampling and data collection

Data collection were conducted by a survey method at various locations within five and four star hotels in six cities and/or locations of India—Jammu, Katra, Srinagar, Gulmarg, Phalgam, and Amritsar. These locations/cities are main tourist destinations of India. In addition, all these four- and five-star hotels are located in these particular cities/locations. Respondents were recruited via nonprobability convenience sampling, an approach used by earlier researchers (Liat et al., 2017; Martinez & Rodriguez Del Bosque, 2013; Parrey, Hakim, & Rather, 2018; Rather, 2018), across different four-star and five-star hotels located in these six cities of India. To screen our respondents, we employed two introductory questions to confirm (a) that the customer had stayed with a particular hotel at least once in the last 12 months, and (b) that the customer was 18 years or over. Questionnaires were distributed to 400 respondents but only 345 fully completed questionnaires were returned. This sample size surpassed the recommended sample size of 150 by Hair, Black, Babin, and Anderson (2010), for a research model with five constructs or fewer, alongside modest communalities (.50) and no under-identified constructs.

This study chose to examine the hospitality (hotel) sector for a number of reasons. First, this sector contributes more toward the growth and development of the country (IBEF, 2018). Second, the naturally high level of interaction between hotel service providers and their customers encourages the occurrence of CBI and CBIL (Bhattacharya & Sen, 2003; Huang et al., 2017). Third, the hospitality industry is specifically suitable because of its high rate of customer retention (Huang et al., 2017).

3.2. Measurements

All constructs were measured with a 7-point Likert-type multiple-item scale, ranging from *strongly disagree* (1) to *strongly agree* (7). Twenty items adapted from the tourism and marketing literature were used to capture the five latent constructs in distributed questionnaire. Specifically, four items measuring CBI that has provided good reliability values were adopted and modified from So et al. (2013). A sample item reads *When someone criticizes this hotel, it feels like a personal insult* (CBI1). Similarly, four items measuring customer satisfaction were adopted from Liat et al. (2017). A sample item reads *Overall I felt satisfied with this hotel* (CS4). Four items measuring affective commitment was adapted from Sui and Baloglu (2003). A sample item reads *I am emotionally attached to this hotel* (AC1). For brand trust, four items were adapted from Martinez and Rodriguez Del Bosque (2013). A sample item reads *I trust on the quality of this hotel* (BT1). Finally, out of four items measuring CBIL, first two items (CBIL1 and CBIL2) and other two items (CBIL3 and CBIL4) were adopted from the studies of Ali et al. (2016) and Liat et al. (2017) respectively. A sample items includes *I intend to keep staying with this hotel* (CBIL1) and *I would encourage friends and relatives to do business with this hotel* (CBIL3). The overall items are reported in Table 2.

The questionnaire has undergone a pretest stage by four hospitality managers and four marketing academics who provided comments about various aspects such as item comprehensibility, wording, ambiguity, and readability (Hair et al., 2010). The questionnaire was tested with 25 participants randomly selected from seven of the chosen hotel brands to ensure that the wording and meaning of the items are comprehensible. Questionnaire was then finalized for data collection.

4. Results

In terms of gender, 52% of respondents were male while 48% were female. In terms of age, 37% of respondents were between 31 and 40 years of age, 27% were between 41 and 50 years, 21% were between 20 and 30 years, and 15% were aged above 51 years. A more complete demographic profile of the respondents is presented in Table 1.

4.1 Testing of measurement model

To assess the measurement model performance, a CFA of the five measured constructs was performed using AMOS by means of maximum likelihood estimation. Data collected were examined through the two-step structural equation modeling (SEM) method (Anderson & Gerbing, 1988). As displayed in Table 2,

Table 1. Demographic and travel behavior of consumers.

Demographics	Number	Percentage		Number	Percentage
Gender			Occupation		
Male	180	52	Business	95	8
Female	165	48	Service	53	15
Age (years)			Professional	121	35
20–30	74	21	Others	76	22
31–40	130	37	Reasons for travelling		
41–50	91	27	Leisure	114	33
Above 51	50	15	Adventure	103	30
Qualification			Religious	87	25
Matriculation	6	2	Business	41	12
Graduation	126	36	Hotel Brand		
Post-graduation	190	55	Four Star	231	67
Others	23	7	Five Star	114	33

Table 2. Results of confirmatory factor analysis.

Construct	SL	TV	M	SD	SMC
Customer brand identification (CBI)					
When someone criticizes this hotel, it feels like a personal insult (CBI1)	.81	18.60	3.06	1.47	.65
When I talk about this hotel, I usually say "we" rather than "they" (CBI2)	.86	20.54	3.95	1.43	.74
This hotel's successes are my successes (CBI3)	.90	22 .24	4.16	1.32	.81
When someone praises this hotel, it feels like a personal compliment (CBI4)	.85	N/A	4.79	1.12	.72
Affective commitment (AC)					
I am emotionally attached to this hotel (AC1)	.92	32.27	4.63	1.26	.84
I feel a strong sense of identification with this hotel (AC2)	.68	15.90	4.72	1.09	.45
The friendliness of the staff in this hotel makes me feel good (AC3)	.91	31.59	4.54	1.24	.83
I enjoy visiting this hotel (AC4)	.95	N/A	4.54	1.24	.89
Brand trust (BT)					
I trust on the quality of this hotel (BT1)	.98	N/A	5.42	1.04	.87
This is an honest hotel (BT2)	.97	54.20	5.46	1.00	.88
The services of this hotel make me feel a sense of security (BT3)	.73	19/15	5.87	.93	.53
I feel that this hotel is interested in its customers (BT4)	.90	34.27	5.47	.94	.80
Customer satisfaction (CS)					
I really enjoyed myself at this hotel (CS1)	.92	32.98	5.09	1.18	.84
I was pleased to do business with this hotel (CS2)	.94	36.25	4.95	1.21	.88
Overall feeling I got from this hotel put me in a good mood (CS3)	.82	23.35	4.89	1.19	.67
Overall I felt satisfied with this hotel (CS4)	.95	N/A	4.99	1.12	.89
Customer behavioral intention of loyalty (CBIL)					
I intend to keep staying with this hotel (CBIL1)	.88	23.67	4.60	1.36	.77
I would recommend this hotel to someone who seeks my advice (CBIL2)	.89	N/A	5.32	1.04	.78
I would encourage friends and relatives to do business with this hotel (CBIL3)	.83	38.65	5.21	1.12	.85
I would say positive things about this hotel to other people (CBIL4)	.94	27.68	5.12	1.16	.86

SL = standard loadings, SMC = squared multiple correlation, M = mean, SD = standard deviation, TV = t-value/critical value, N/A = not applicable

the overall CFA goodness-of-fit indices were indicated to be satisfactory (CFI, TLI, GFI, and NFI >.90; RMSEA <.08; Bentler & Bonnett, 1980), with the overall CFA measurement model attaining an excellent fit ($\chi 2$ = 572.540, df = 197, $\chi 2$/ df = 2.906, p < .0001, CFI = .96; NFI = .94, TLI = .95, GFI = .88, RMSEA = .074, SRMR = .047).

4.2. Convergent validity testing

In addition, CFA was utilized to assess the reliability and validity of all scale items. Applying the conditions suggested by Fornell and Larcker (1981), convergent validity was confirmed. All CFA factor loadings were significant at $p < .001$ (Table 2).

4.3. Reliability testing

Reliabilities for each of the construct were above the value of .70, fulfilling the general condition of reliability for the research instruments (Hair et al., 2010). Cronbach's alpha values of the constructs ranged from .91 to .95, all of which are higher than the commonly recommended value of .70. With regards to composite reliability, the values varied from .91 to.95, above the recommended cutoff value of .70 (Fornell & Larcker, 1981). Values are presented in Table 3.

4.4. Discriminant validity testing

In line with Fornell and Larcker (1981)'s suggested guidelines for discriminant validity, the correlations among the constructs were evaluated with the square root of each construct's AVE. Discriminant validity of the constructs was supported because the average extracted variances of all constructs range between .854 and .909, which are above the suggested value of 0.5, as presented in Table 3

4.5. Findings and testing of the structural model

The hypothesis-testing SEM results of the five constructs are presented in Tables 4 and 5. The structural model has been tested using AMOS via maximum likelihood estimation, which showed the model to have a good model fit with overall model fitness indices to be $\chi2 = 640.338$, df = 200, $\chi2/df = 3.202$, CFI = .94, TLI = .94, NFI = .93, GFI = .87, RMSEA = .080, and SRMR = .064.

Statistically significant results with large effect sizes were found for the positive influence of CBI on affective commitment ($\beta = .40$, $R^2 = .81$, $p < .0001$), customer satisfaction ($\beta = .79$, $R^2 = .62$, $p < .0001$), brand trust ($\beta = .20$, $R^2 = .53$, $p < .01$), and CBIL ($\beta = .29$, $R^2 = .80$, $p < .0001$), supporting H1, H2, H3, and H4.

Table 3. Measure correlations, reliability, and average variance extracted.

Construct	α	CR	AVE	CBIL	CBI	CS	AC	BT
CBIL	.965	.945	.767	**.872**				
CBI	.924	.917	.743	.803	**.864**			
CS	.939	.950	.826	.816	.786	**.896**		
AC	.942	.925	.767	.820	.833	.853	**.860**	
BT	.934	.944	.819	.791	.641	.718	.713	**.889**

α = Cronbach's alpha, CR = construct reliability, AVE = average variance extracted, CBIL = Customer behavioral intention of loyalty, CBI = customer brand identification, BT = brand trust, CS = customer satisfaction, AC = affective commitment.

Off diagonal factors are the correlations among the study constructs. The bold diagonal variables are the square root of the variance shared among the research constructs and its measures.

Table 4. Structural equation model results.

		R^2	β	t-value	Supported	Direct Effects	Indirect Effects	Total Effects
H1	CBI → AC	.81	.40	7.3	Yes	.39	.43	.83
H2	CBI → CS	.62	.79	16.5	Yes	.78	–	.78
H3	CBI → BT	.53	.20	2.8	Yes	.20	.44	.64
H4	CBI → CBIL	.80	.29	4.6	Yes	.28	.51	.80
H5	CS → AC	.81	.44	7.7	Yes	.43	.08	.51
H6	CS → CBIL	.80	.21	3.2	Yes	.20	.27	.48
H7	BT → AC	.81	.14	3.4	Yes	.14	–	.14
H8	BT → CBIL	.80	.35	7.8	Yes	.34	.02	.36
H9	AC → CBIL	.80	.16	2.75	Yes	.15	–	.15

The overall model fitness indices: χ2 = 640.338, df = 200, χ2/df = 3.202, CFI = .94, TLI = .94, NFI = .93, GFI = .87, RMSEA = .080, and SRMR = .064 reflect good model fit.

Table 5. Mediation effects.

Independent variable	Mediator variable	Dependent variable	Mediated effect	Total effect	Direct effect	Indirect effect
CBI	CS, BT, AC	CBIL	Full Mediation	.86	.39	.47

Model fitness indices: χ2 = 595.483, df = 198, χ2/df = 3 .007, CFI = .95, TLI = .95, NFI = .94, GFI = .87, RMSEA = .07, SRMR = .06

Customer satisfaction in turn demonstrated a statistically significant and medium-sized positive influence on affective commitment (β = .44, R^2 = .81, p < .0001), supporting H5, and a smaller but statistically significant positive influence on CBIL (β = .21, R^2 = .80, p < .0001), supporting H6. Brand trust demonstrated statistically significant positive influence on affective commitment (β = .14, R^2 = .81, p < .0001) and CBIL (β = .35, R^2 = .80, p < .0001), supporting H7 and H8, respectively. Affective commitment was found to have a statistically significant impact on CBIL (β = .16, R^2 = .80, p < .05), supporting H9. It is important to note that all the nine hypotheses were supported and hence accepted.

4.6. Mediating effects of affective commitment, customer satisfaction, and brand trust

To examine the mediating effects of affective commitment, customer satisfaction, and brand trust on CBIL, the study evaluated the direct, indirect, and total effects. An estimating analysis as suggested by Brown (1997) was used to examine the mediation effects in a SEM framework. Mediation occurs when an independent variable influences a dependent variable directly and also indirectly through another variable (mediator). This study tested the influence of CBI (independent variable) on CBIL (dependent variable) through affective commitment, customer satisfaction, and brand trust (mediators). CBI has a statistically significant indirect impact on CBIL through the three mediators (β = .47, p < .0001) as shown in Table 5, supporting H10. In the overall model, the indirect influence of CBI on CBIL is the strongest (β = .51) followed by the indirect influences (via affective commitment) of customer satisfaction (β = .27) and brand trust on CBIL (β = .023), as presented in Table 5.

4.7. Testing the nonmediated alternate model

A nonmediated alternate model was also tested (e.g. Morgan & Hunt, 1994) to verify the validity and robustness of the proposed research model (Kelloway, 1998). The overall fitness of the nonmediated model was poorer compared to the overall fitness of the proposed research model (GFI = .77, CMIN/DF = 6.766, CFI = .87, RMSEA = .12, SRMR = .47). The explained variances were also smaller than those of the proposed model (e.g. 73% versus 80% in CBIL).

5. Conclusion and implications

5.1. Conclusion

This study contributes to customer behavior and social identification literature in marketing, particularly in the hospitality context. This study is the first to have simultaneously examined the relationships among CBI, affective commitment, customer satisfaction, brand trust, and CBIL, having developed and empirically tested an integrated model that comprehensively assessed these relationships. Therefore, this research sought to develop and test a theoretical model of CBI and customer satisfaction effects on a specific set of customer-based variables, including brand trust, affective commitment, and CBIL.

Overall, our empirical results offered support for all our hypotheses, thus empirically corroborating CBI and customer satisfaction's importance for companies seeking to increase these customer-based outcomes. As such, this study builds on an emerging literature stream that takes a *social-identity theory* of CBI (Fujita et al., 2018; Martinez & Rodriguez Del Bosque, 2014; Tuskej & Podnar, 2018) and *relationship marketing theory* of customer satisfaction, brand trust, and affective commitment (Liat et al., 2017; Rather, 2018; Van Tonder & Petzer, 2018), and contributes to it by empirically testing and validating our proposed conceptual model vis-à-vis an associated alternative model. Overall, we find that CBI and customer satisfaction can be used as a catalyst to drive brand trust, which in turn helps to increase affective commitment and CBIL in hospitality context. Thus, this study extended the concept of CBIL and its antecedents in hospitality context, contributing to services marketing generally and contemporary hospitality and tourism management literature particularly.

In marketing literature, there is a plethora of research on CBI and CBIL carried out in sectors such as B2B contexts (Keh & Xie, 2009), product categories of mobile phones and television settings (Elbedweihy et al., 2016), mobile phones, athletic shoes, soft drinks, and groceries (Stokburger-Sauer et al., 2012), restaurant settings (Huang et al., 2017), online social media (Fujita et al., 2018), as well as tourism destination branding (Kumar & Kaushik, 2017) with relatively unexplored and limited insights focusing on hospitality (hotel) service providers. Thus, this study's development and validation of a structural model and the tests of interdependencies among the constructs in the hospitality/hotel sector offer a new twist to the literature.

5.2. Theoretical implications

The theoretical model confirms that customer brand identification is the expansion of social identification-informed lens and satisfaction, brand trust, and affective commitment, is the expansion of relationship marketing domain (Fujita et al., 2018; Rather, 2018; Van Tonder & Petzer, 2018). Previous research acknowledges the antecedent effect of customer satisfaction, brand trust, perceived value, and affective commitment on CBIL (Han & Hyun, 2017; Mattila, 2006; So et al., 2013; Sui & Baloglu, 2003). Therefore, this study findings further provide existing knowledge by offering more insight into the extent to which the social identity and relationship marketing-based factors contributing to CBIL.

Theoretically, our analyses contribute to the development of SIT/RMT-based insight by uncovering key effects of CBI, customer satisfaction, brand trust, and affective commitment on ensuing CBIL for four and five-star hotels, thereby directly responding to Kandampully et al., (2015) call for further research on customer loyalty dynamics within the hospitality sector. Although SIT and RMT-based findings are typically proposed in isolation, our integrative analyses provide insight into their combined effect. Therefore, using SIT and RMT as a lens to examine customer brand identification and loyalty was established to be useful. The findings show that strong customer–brand relationships are based on customers' identification with the firm, which help them satisfy one or more important self-definitional needs and motivates them to engage in favorable as well as potentially unfavorable company-related behaviors (Bhattacharya & Sen, 2003; He et al., 2012). Therefore, our findings reveal that the development of customers' brand-related identification, trust, and commitment is conducive to fostering their ensuing customer behavioral loyalty by undertaking more (extensive) brand-related activities (Hollebeek et al., 2016; Rather, 2018). In addition, these concepts are also conducive to attitudinal loyalty development in hospitality, such as by posting favorable hotel-related reviews on TripAdvisor.

Therefore, motivating customers to engage in brand-related activities represents a strategic priority for marketers. For luxury hotels, these customer activities may include requesting a room upgrade, discussing the hotel with their family and friends, liking or following the hotel's social media pages, or undertaking hotel-related self-service (e.g. by booking a room online; Hollebeek et al., 2016; Tuskej & Podnar, 2018). Correspondingly, our findings suggest a positive effect of CBI, satisfaction, commitment, and trust on the development of CBIL for star hotels in the emerging market context. Furthermore, based on SIT, customers are keener to identify with those brands that help them maintain or enhance their self-esteem (Bhattacharya & Sen, 2003; Tuskej & Podnar, 2018). Hence, it is vital for brands to invest in offering exceptional product quality that aligns with customers' needs and values, thus driving heightened customer brand identification, which in turn is expected to foster greater customer behavioral intention of loyalty.

5.3. Managerial implications

From a practical perspective, the results also offer many implications for hospitality firms in developing lasting and strong relationships with their customers.

First, developing and maintaining customer relationships have received considerable attention from managerial perspectives (Elbedweihy et al., 2016; Huang et al., 2017; Martinez & Rodriguez Del Bosque, 2014). This study indicates that loyalty intentions have varying degrees of influence and/or sensitivity to brand trust followed by CBI, customer satisfaction, and affective commitment. Brand trust has a much stronger influence on loyalty intentions compared to affective commitment and hence, marketing practitioners should identify the fundamental role of brand trust in influencing customers' patronage, recommendation behaviors, and intentions to revisit. Thus, the potency of relationship between trust and loyalty intentions in the present model highlights the need for hoteliers to portray their services as trustworthy, reliable, and respectful, such as keeping promises made to customers, protecting customers' information, as well to ensuring customers' confidentiality. These practices will increase customer confidence in hotel management and provide opportunity for word-of-mouth recommendations to others (Keh & Xie, 2009; Martinez & Rodriguez Del Bosque, 2013). Therefore, trust has been identified as a key factor in building a long-term favorable relationship between customers and hotel service providers (brand). To influence the level of trust among current and potential customers, hospitality marketers should also focus on relationship-building practices instead of employing transactional marketing tactics and/or strategies. For instance, marketers have been successful in instilling an emotional bond toward the "Costco" brand, the second-largest retailer in the United States. Costco has effectively showcased its care about its customers by emphasizing that it pays "living wages" to its employees (Kumar & Kaushik, 2017). Similarly, hospitality marketers can nurture and build brand trust among current and potential customers by highlighting their caring attitude with their customers, employees, and society at large. Hospitality marketers are also needed to deliver a consistent performance by communicating characteristics that are valued by their target segment.

Second, the significant positive effects of CBI suggest that companies may invest in CBI. Instead of just focusing on brand awareness, brand investment may lead to developing strong identification meaning to customers so that it helps customers search for customer brand bond and/or relationship. This study noticed the effects of CBI on customer satisfaction, brand trust, affective commitment and CBIL, and such results reinforce the importance of developing strong CBI, since a brand (hotel) with a strong identification and/or identity increases customer's perception of social exchange relationships and influences hotel–customer loyalty. Therefore, hospitality managers may not only integrate their rational social exchange investment, but also investment on customer–social interaction. Brand community would be a feasible tool for developing sound customer identification (He et al., 2012). Hence, CBI can occur not only through the fostering of interactions between brand and customer due to a myriad of approaches, from event marketing to product cocreation, but also through interactions among customers around a brand, due to brand communities, both virtual and physical (He et al., 2012; Stokburger-Sauer et al., 2012; Tuskej & Podnar, 2018). Relatedly, hospitality managers and firms may also increase customer identification, affective commitment, and loyalty through several strategies. For example, public relations, advertising, and marketing campaigns can act as key tools to further influence the customer's perception (Kumar & Kaushik, 2017). The same goes for public activities such as sponsorships, charity works, social campaigns, and other corporate social responsibility activities (He et al., 2012; Martinez & Rodriguez Del Bosque, 2013; Stokburger-Sauer et al., 2012).

Third, customer satisfaction was found to have large positive effect on CBIL through affective commitment. The findings of this study are in line with other prior research conducted in the hotel sector, whereby customers who are satisfied with the services rendered by the hotel would turn out to be loyal customers (Liat et al., 2017; Tanford, 2016). The findings confirmed the RMT-informed perspective that customer satisfaction has a positive influence on loyalty. Loyalty is a valuable asset for a firm, particularly in the highly competitive hospitality sector. As the cost of successfully attracting a new customer is 6–15 times costlier than that of sustaining an existing one, hospitality managers have to adopt marketing approaches that increase customer satisfaction. Achieving and maintaining customer loyalty is crucial in the hospitality (including hotel) sector. Given that the cost of attracting new customers is significantly higher than that of retaining current ones (Huang et al., 2017; Reichheld & Sasser, 1990), managers are forever looking to identify ways to stimulate customer retention and increase their lifetime value (Rather, 2018). For instance, suggestion or feedback programs should be underlined by most hotels, as this method can facilitate them to identify any weak areas that need improvement in their operation. This can be performed with the use of survey forms distributed either through e-mail or at the front desk. Effective strategies will translate customer satisfaction into customer loyalty as well as attract potential customers.

Fourth, satisfaction has a positive and significant influence on affective commitment of customers. Hospitality providers should cautiously handle customer expectations. Due to the intangibility of service offerings and competitiveness of the hospitality sector, it is generally easy for hoteliers to stumble into this trap of inflating customer expectations to retain and acquire business. As satisfaction has a positive and significant influence on both customers' affective commitment and loyalty, the inability of hospitality service providers to meet customer expectations would negatively impact affective commitment and customers' intentions repeated patronage and/or recommendations. Thus, the strength of the relationship among customer satisfaction, affective commitment, and loyalty in the model recommends hospitality management to continuously invest in monitoring and measuring satisfaction performance.

Fifth, a positive impact of affective commitment on loyalty intentions was found. They have to provide personalized services to meet customer's needs where necessary. For example, Mattila (2006) echoed that affective commitment is an essential predictor of loyalty, established through the development of emotional bonds with customers. Customers with greater affective commitment with a hotel brand would likely consider that hotel brand as their first choice and promote the hotel brand among their friends and relatives.

Sixth, brand rust has a direct impact on affective commitment. The empirical results demonstrate that trust emerges to be an essential driver of affective commitment in developing deeper, valuable, and important relationships with customers. Hence, affective commitment is an essential inclusion in this study model: it relates to emotional bonds and enduring relationships. The current findings are consistent with the findings of earlier research, whereby brand trust plays a role in developing affective commitment and increasing positive behaviors (Morgan & Hunt, 1994; Van Tonder & Petzer, 2018).

Finally, the findings indicate positive mediating effects of affective commitment, customer satisfaction, and brand trust of the relationship between CBI and CBIL.

These suggest that brand identification helps to create loyal customers if the initiatives satisfy their desired end states. Given that affective commitment, customer satisfaction, and brand trust considerably mediate the influence of identification on brand success, firms are advised not to solely focus on identity-based marketing strategies. Instead, a balanced mix of marketing activities aiming at identification, commitment, trust, and customer satisfaction seems promising.

5.4. Limitations and future research studies

Irrespective of theoretical and practical implications, this study is not without limitations. First, the study adopted cross-sectional data. Although similar to previous studies, this approach means that the findings can only suggest an association among these constructs instead of a causal relationship. Therefore, longitudinal study could be adopted to assess the interrelationship of constructs to generalize results.

Second, the study was conducted only on one country (India) and a single sector (four- and five-star hotels) as context. Therefore, future research can replicate the estimated relationships across different sectors, industries, or countries. Third, the role of demographic variables such as gender, income, and age are not considered in this study. Assessing the impact of these factors on the proposed research framework will be a meaningful extension in future research.

Finally, one more valuable undertaking for future examination will be to identify other determinants and/or antecedents of CBI and CBIL such as the emergent themes of social benefits, brand identity, customer engagement behaviors, brand prestige, value cocreation, brand distinctiveness, corporate social responsibility, memorable brand experience, value congruence, corporate reputation, and brand attractiveness (Hollebeek et al., 2016; Rather, 2018; Sharma & Rather, 2015; Tuskej & Podnar, 2018)

Acknowledgments

The authors would like to thank The Business School, University of Jammu and hospitality sector for providing necessary assistance and help in data collection.

Disclosure statement

No potential conflict of interest was reported by the authors.

ORCID

Raouf Ahmad Rather (iD) http://orcid.org/0000-0002-9242-1165

References

Ali, F., Ryu, K., & Hussain, K. (2016). Influence of experiences on memories, satisfaction and behavioral intentions: A study of creative tourism. *Journal of Travel & Tourism Marketing, 33* (1), 85–100.

Allen, N. J., & Meyer, J. P. (1990). The measurement and antecedents of affective, continuance and normative commitment to the organization. *Journal of Occupational Psychology, 63*(1), 1–18.

Anderson, J. C., & Gerbing, D. W. (1988). Structural equation modelling in practice: A review and recommended two-step approach. *Psychological Bulletin, 103*(3), 411–423.

Ashforth, B. E., & Mael, F. (1989). Social identity theory and the organization. *Academy of Management Review, 14*, 20–39.

Bentler, P. M., & Bonnett, D. G. (1980). Significance tests and goodness of fit in the analysis of covariance structures. *Psychological Bulletin, 88*(3), 588–606.

Berry, L. L. (1983). Relationship marketing. In L. L. Berry, G. L. Shostack, & G. D. Upah (Eds.), *Emerging perspectives on services marketing* (pp. 25–28). Chicago, IL: American Marketing Association.

Berry, L. L., & Parasuraman, A. (1991). *Marketing services*. New York, NY: Free Press.

Bhattacharya, C. B., & Sen, S. (2003). Customer company identification: A framework for understanding customers relationships with companies. *Journal of Marketing, 67*(2), 76–88.

Brodie, R. (2017). Enhancing theory development in the domain of relationship marketing: How to avoid the danger of getting stuck in the middle. *Journal of Services Marketing, 31* (1), 20–23.

Brown, R. L. (1997). Assessing specific mediational effects in complex theoretical models, structural equation modeling. *Multidisciplinary Journal, 4*(2), 142–156.

Chen, C. F., & Chen, F. S. (2010). Experience quality, perceived value, satisfaction and behavioral intentions for heritage tourists. *Tourism Management, 31*(1), 29–35.

Curth, S., Uhrich, S., & Benkenstein, M. (2014). How commitment to fellow customers affects the customer- firm relationship and customer citizenship behavior. *Journal of Services Marketing, 28*(2), 147–158.

Elbedweihy, A., Jayawardhena, C., Elsharnouby, M. H., & Elsharnouby, T. H. (2016). Customer relationship building: The role of brand attractiveness and customer-brand identification. *Journal of Business Research, 69*, 2901–2910.

Escalas, J. E., & Bettman, J. R. (2003). You are what they eat: The influence of reference groups on customers connections to brands. *Journal of Customer Psychology, 13*(3), 339–348.

Fornell, C., & Larcker, D. F. (1981). Evaluating structural equation models with unobservable variables and measurement error. *Journal of Marketing Research, 18*(1), 39–50.

Fujita, M., Harrigan, P., & Soutar, G. N. (2018). Capturing and co-creating student experiences in social media: A social identity theory perspective. *Journal of Marketing Theory and Practice, 26*(1–2), 55–71.

Fullerton, G. (2003). When does commitment lead to loyalty? *Journal of Service Research, 5*(4), 333–344.

Geyskens, I., Steenkamp, J. E. M., Scheer, L. K., & Kumar, N. (1996). The effects of trust and interdependence on relationship commitment: A trans-Atlantic study. *International Journal of Research in Marketing, 13*, 303–317.

Grönroos, C. (1994). From marketing mix to relationship marketing: Towards a paradigm shift in marketing. *Management Decision, 32*(2), 4–20.

Hair, J. F., Black, W. C., Babin, B. J., & Anderson, R. E. (2010). *Multivariate data analysis: A global perspective* (Vol. 7). Upper Saddle River, NJ: Pearson.

Han, H., & Hyun, S. S. (2017). Impact of hotel-restaurant image and quality of physical-environment, service, and food on satisfaction and intention. *International Journal of Hospitality Management, 63*, 82–92.

He, H., & Li, Y. (2010). CSR and service brand: The mediating effect of brand identification and moderating effect of service quality. *Journal of Business Ethics, 100*, 673–688.

He, H., Li, Y., & Harris, L. (2012). Social identity perspective on brand loyalty. *Journal of Business Research, 65*, 648–657.

Hennig-Thurau, T., Gwinner, K. P., & Gremler, D. D. (2002). Understanding relationship marketing outcomes: An integration of relational benefits and relationship quality. *Journal of Service Research, 4*(3), 230–247.

Hollebeek, L., Srivastava, R. K., & Chen, T. (2016). S-D logic-informed customer engagement: Integrative framework, revised fundamental propositions, and application to CRM. *Journal of the Academy of Marketing Science*. Online First. doi: 10.1007/s11747-016-0494-5

Huang, M. H., Cheng, Z. H., & Chen, I. C. (2017). The importance of CSR in forming customer-company identification and long-term loyalty. *Journal of Services Marketing, 31*(1), 63–72.

IBEF. (2018). Tourism & hospitality industry in india. Retrieved from https://www.ibef.org/industry/tourism-hospitality-india.aspx

Kandampully, J., Zhang, T., & Bilgihan, A. (2015). Customer loyalty: A review and future directions with a special focus on the hospitality industry. *International Journal of Contemporary Hospitality Management, 27*(3), 379–414.

Keh, H. T., & Xie, Y. (2009). Corporate reputation and customer behavioral intentions: The role of trust, identification and commitment. *Industrial Marketing Management, 38*, 732–742.

Kelloway, E. K. (1998). *Using LISREL for structural equation modeling: A researcher's guide.* London: Sage.

Kumar, V., & Kaushik, A. K. (2017). Achieving destination advocacy and destination loyalty through destination brand identification. *Journal of Travel & Tourism Marketing, 34*(9), 1247–1260.

Lam, S. K., Ahearne, M., Mullins, R., Hayati, B., & Schillewaert, N. (2013). Exploring the dynamics of antecedents to customer–Brand identification with a new brand. *Journal of the Academy of Marketing Science, 41*(2), 234–252.

Liat, C. B., Mansori, S., Chuan, G. C., & Imrie, B. C. (2017). Hotel service recovery and service quality: Influences of corporate image and generational differences in the relationship between customer satisfaction and loyalty. *Journal of Global Marketing, 30*(1), 42–51.

Martinez, P., & Rodriguez Del Bosque, I. (2013). CSR and customer loyalty: The roles of trust, customer identification with the company and satisfaction. *International Journal of Hospitality Management, 35*, 89–99.

Martinez, P., & Rodriguez Del Bosque, I. (2014). Exploring the antecedents of hotel customer loyalty: A social identity perspective. *Journal of Hospitality Marketing & Management, 24*(1), 1–23.

Mattila, A. S. (2006). How affective commitment boosts guest loyalty (and promotes frequent-guest programs). *Cornell Hotel and Restaurant Administration Quarterly, 47*(2), 174–181.

Morgan, R., & Hunt, S. (1994). The commitment-trust theory of relationship marketing. *Journal of Marketing, 58*, 20–38.

Oliver, R. L. (1997). *Satisfaction: A behavioral perspective on the customer.* New York: McGraw-Hill.

Parrey, S. H., Hakim, I. A., & Rather, R. A. (2018). Mediating role of government initiatives and media influence between perceived risks and destination image: A study of conflict zone. *International Journal of Tourism Cities.* doi:10.1108/IJTC-02-2018-0019.

PRNewswire. (2016). The global luxury hotels market to 2019. Retrieved from https://www.radiantinsights.com/research/the-global-luxury-hotels-market-to-2019

Rather, R. A. (2017). Investigating the impact of customer brand identification on hospitality brand loyalty: A social identity perspective. *Journal of Hospitality Marketing & Management, 27*(5), 487–513.

Rather, R. A. (2018). Consequences of consumer engagement in service marketing: An empirical exploration. *Journal of Global Marketing*, 1–20. (In press).

Rather, R. A., & Parray, S. H. (2018). Customer engagement in increasing affective commitment within hospitality sector. *Journal of Hospitality Application & Research, 13*(1), 73–91.

Rather, R. A., & Sharma, J. (2016a). Brand loyalty with hospitality brands: The role of customer brand identification, brand satisfaction and brand commitment. *Pacific Business Review International, 1*(3), 76–86.

Rather, R. A., & Sharma, J. (2016b). Customer engagement in strengthening customer loyalty in hospitality sector. *South Asian Journal of Tourism and Heritage, 9*(2), 62–81.

Rather, R. A., & Sharma, J. (2017). Customer engagement for evaluating customer relationships in hotel industry. *European Journal of Tourism, Hospitality and Recreation, 8*(1), 1–13.

Rather, R. A., & Sharma, J. (2018). The effects of customer satisfaction and commitment on customer loyalty: Evidence from the hotel industry. *Journal of Hospitality Application & Research, 12*(2), 41–60.

Reichheld, F. F., & Sasser, J. W. (1990). Zero defections: Quality comes to services. *Harvard Business Review, 68*(5), 105–111.

Sharma, J., & Rather, R. A. (2015). Understanding the customer experience: An exploratory study of "A" category hotels. *International Journal on Customer Relations, 3*(2), 21–31.

Sharma, J., & Rather, R. A. (2016). The role of customer engagement in ensuring sustainable development in hospitality sector. *International Journal of Hospitality & Tourism Systems, 9* (1), 33–43.

Shukla, P., Banerjee, M., & Singh, J. (2016). Customer commitment to luxury brands: Antecedents and consequences. *Journal of Business Research, 69*(1), 323–331.

So, K. K. F., King, C., Sparks, B., & Wang, Y. (2013). The influence of customer brand identification on hotel brand evaluation and loyalty development. *International Journal of Hospitality Management, 34*, 31–41.

Stokburger-Sauer, N., Ratneshwar, S., & Sen, S. (2012). Drivers of customer–Brand identification. *International Journal of Research in Marketing, 29*(4), 406–418.

Su, L., Swanson, S. R., Chinchanachokchai, S., Hsu, M. K., & Chen, X. (2016). Reputation and intentions: The role of satisfaction, identification, and commitment. *Journal of Business Research, 69*(9), 3261–3269.

Sui, J. S., & Baloglu, S. (2003). The role of emotional commitment in relationship marketing: An empirical investigation of a loyalty model for casinos. *Journal of Hospitality and Tourism Research, 27*, 470–489.

Tajfel, H., & Turner, J. C. (1986). The social identity theory of inter-group behavior. In S. Worchel & L. W. Austin (Eds.), *Psychology of intergroup relations* (pp. 7–24). Chicago, IL: Nelson-Hall.

Tanford, S. (2016). Antecedents and outcomes of hospitality loyalty: A meta-analysis. *Cornell Hospitality Quarterly, 57*(2), 122–137.

Tuskej, U., Golob, U., & Podnar, K. (2013). The role of customer-brand identification in building brand relationships. *Journal of Business Research, 66*, 53–59.

Tuskej, U., & Podnar, K. (2018). Customers' identification with corporate brands: Brand prestige, anthropomorphism and engagement in social media. *Journal of Product & Brand Management, 27*(1), 3–17.

UNWTO. (2017). Tourism highlights. Retried from http://mkt.unwto.org/publication/unwtotour ism-highlights

Van Tonder, E., & Petzer, D. J. (2018). The interrelationships between relationship marketing constructs and customer engagement dimensions. *The Service Industries Journal*, 1–26.

Vesel, P., & Zabkar, V. (2010). Relationship quality evaluation in retailers' relationships with consumers. *European Journal of Marketing, 44*(9–10), 1334–1365.

Hotel's best practices as strategic drivers for environmental sustainability and green marketing

Chindu Chandran (ID) and Prodyut Bhattacharya (ID)

ABSTRACT

Majority of the hospitality industry depends on the natural beauty and charisma of destinations thus emphasis on sustainability should be laid. Hotel operators are aware of the benefits of sustainability and many of them publicly promote their best practices as their marketing strategy. They are adopting green marketing as an opportunity to differentiate themselves from their competitors, cut costs associated with waste disposal and material usage. This paper aims at understanding the importance of green marketing with respect to implementing green practices in the hotel industry. The purpose of the study was to determine the benefits and challenges of undertaking environmental best practices and integrating these practices into their marketing strategy. The data were gathered from both primary and secondary sources. Primary data were collected by surveying the hotel staff across 20 hotels in India. Study concluded that hotels who have implemented green practices in their operations have been benefited like enhanced reputation and more worth among customers in comparison to other hotels. Most of the hotel implemented the environmental initiatives without any systematic approach. It is recommended that hotels should develop green management policies for improved quality of the environment and minimizing their impact of operations on the environment.

酒店行业最佳实践对环境可持续与绿色营销的战略性驱动

可持续发展, 又称"绿色发展", 已迅速成为酒店行业发展的主流态势。当前, 酒店行业和旅游业的发展大都依靠于目的地的自然风光和独特魅力。

酒店的经营者们意识到了可持续发展具有的潜在效益, 其中, 许多从业者已经将它作为营销策略的一部分, 向大众宣传其最佳实践。他们利用绿色营销活动从行业竞争中脱颖, 同时减少废物处理和物料消耗成本。

本文旨在了解关于酒店行业推行环保实践这一绿色营销的重要性。该研究的目的在于确定环保最佳实践及将这些实践与行业营销策略整合带来的效益与挑战。

本研究所搜集的数据包括原始数据和二手数据两种。原始数据收集整理于向印度20家酒店员工的调查访问。研究结果显示: 在运营中实行绿色实践的酒店较其他酒店, 声誉有所提高, 在客户中也更具价值; 此外, 大部分的酒店在环保倡议的实际推行中未采取系统性措施。建议酒店行业制定绿色管理政策, 提高环境质量, 使经营活动对环境的影响最小化。

1. Introduction

Green marketing was defined as "the way to conceive exchange relationships that goes beyond the current needs of the consumers, considering at the same time the social interest in protecting the natural environment" (Chamorro & Bañegil, 2006; Dangelico et. al, 2017; Singh et. al, 2012; Soonthonsmai, 2007). The demand for sustainable development and green marketing is achieving its momentum greatly due to a recent growth in environmental concerns among the communities over the last few decades (Chen & Chang, 2012; Jhawar et al., 2012; Leonidou, Leonidou, Fotiadis, & Zeriti, 2013). The goal of sustainability is depicted as a development that includes formulating a social and economic system which must be incorporated within environmental concerns (Griffin & Prakash, 2010; Kinoti, 2011; Saadatian, Haw, Mat, & Sopian, 2012). The development and success of the hotel industry majorly depend on the availability of natural resources around them and how they utilize it. The natural resources of a destination are one of the significant marketing points of the local hotel industry. On the other hand, hotels are among some of the chief consumers of energy, water resources and consequently generate a large amount of waste.

With the emerging market of green consumers, the business landscape for hoteliers is also changing. To meet the demands of green consumers, hotels are largely adopting to sustainable marketing practices and pushing themselves toward responsibility (Mensah, 2004; Papadas, Avlonitis, & Carrigan, 2017; Rathod, 2014; Sert, 2017). Hotels are the major part of the hospitality industry that contributes maximum share in profits but at the same time, there is an inevitable link between hotels and environmental issues (Swarbrooke, 1999). With the changing environment, consumer's tastes and preferences have also changed and this change is very well reflected even in the hospitality sector. Today hotels are involved in various green practices, but hoteliers adopt these practices without knowing the benefits and background knowledge about these practices. In specific, hotels have also adopted various green marketing strategies to respond to the emerging environmental issues (Li, Wang, & Yu, 2015; Zhang & Yang, 2016). Chan (2008) calls these strategies as environmental management systems (EMSs) which include strategies such as efficient use of energy, water and material resources in all aspects of the hotels' operations. To recognize the efforts that hotels are making to successfully implement their green marketing strategies, various awards and certifications are given. This is a form of appreciation for their contributions and serves as motivation for the others to progress toward such green commitments.

The philosophy of green marketing differentiates it from traditional marketing as green marketing explains that it is not only about understanding the commercial advantage or profit exchange relationship but it also includes the organization's relationship with society and environment in general (Chamorro & Banegil, 2006; Geerts, 2014). The effort to implement green marketing is not only the duty of the marketing department but it involves the entire organization with different functional areas such as quality, design, production and supplies. The development of green marketing evolves through the process of planning, implementation and control on a policy of systems, processes and product and promotion with the main objectives to minimize the impact on the natural environment and its conservation and protection (Eneizaan et. al., 2016).

It is observed that hotels are striving and finding hard times to incorporate the best practices into their daily operation while it is a challenge for them to cater the needs of green consumers with reference to sustainable practices (Barbulescu, 2017; Berry, 1980; Zeithaml, Parasuraman, & Berry, 1985). The reason why hotels hesitate to adopt green practices is generally the consideration of short-term profit and the high costs of investments. It has been reported that customers show a positive intention to visit those hotels that adopt green practices than preferring hotels that do not employ them (Fukrey et al., 2014; Gao et al., 2014; Ham & Choi, 2012). However, when the customers find the green claims are fake or forged, the trust toward the organization gets affected (Bhaskaran, 2006; Caputa, 2015). These types of claims are called "greenwashing" (Rahman et al., 2015; Sinnappan & Rahman, 2011). If hoteliers want to cater to the demands of the green segments, greenwashing must be avoided which is one of the greatest challenges they are facing.

Thus, the overall objective was to examine the role of adoption of best practices for green marketing in the hotel industry in India. The specific objectives of the study were:

    I. to determine the drivers for adoption of best practices for green marketing by hotels;
   II. to explore the benefits and challenges associated with the adoption of best practices for green marketing by hotels;
  III. to find out the best practices implemented by hotels for green marketing.

The objective of the paper is to focus on the roles that the hoteliers can perform in the preservation of the natural environment by incorporating various green practices into their operations and thus highlighting their practices by green marketing. This study will be beneficial mainly to the hoteliers as the discussion provides some insights about the importance and ways to perform best practices in their daily operations which could also serve as a tool to market their initiatives as green marketing initiatives. Besides that, understanding the challenges of this concept will also help them in strategizing their advertising tactics to focus on the green market. Thus, hoteliers can pay attention to all the risks that can occur due to their business operations so as not to damage the environment.

2. Methodology

The aim of the study was to examine the best practices being practised by the hotels and to identify the drivers and challenges of adopting the green practices. This study adopted a descriptive cross-sectional research method which employed a self-administered and closed-ended questionnaire to survey owners, marketing managers etc. in the hotel industry. Issues of confidentiality were taken into consideration and interviewees were assured that the data would be kept confidential and that the names of the interviewees, as well as hotel, would not be mentioned.

2.1. Sampling

The participants selected in this study shared a common feature that they were directly related to the functioning of the hotel operations, that is the owner, marketing managers, general managers and other staff members of hotels. Twenty hotels were surveyed in May 2016–April 2017 in India and the selected hotels which were located around the protected areas included all categories small, medium and large hotels. These hotels are spread throughout the country in both urban and rural areas. Purposive sampling was employed to determine the sample. General managers were interviewed as they possess knowledge of all the policies and environmentally friendly practices within their hotels. To assess the performance level of green practices by the hotels, it was critical and essential that the employees be familiar with green practices at work by performing and observing them.

2.2. Data collection

Secondary data were collected by means of an extensive literature study that included textbooks, journal articles and the hotel websites etc. Semi-structured interviews were used to collect data for this study from a sample comprising managers and other hotel staff. To examine these areas of interest, a total of 20 detailed structured questionnaires were administered to selected hotels from the various geographical location of the country and not from the commercial luxury property. A structured questionnaire was prepared consisting of closed-ended questions to elicit information from respondents. The ordinal scale used was based on semantic differential scaled-response questions according to a five-point Likert-type scale (ranging from "strongly agree" to "strongly disagree"). The first part of the questionnaire sought to collect general information about the hotel. Following data variables were included: industry type; employment size; position occupied; functional area employed; the number of years involved in green practices; ethnic group; and age. Second part collected information on drivers for adopting green marketing practices. The third and fourth part aimed at obtaining data on the benefits of adopting green marketing and the challenges of adopting green marketing respectively. To know about the best practices being practised by the hotels, interview questions were developed to determine the best practice of the operator of the resorts. The questionnaire contained several questions based on the area of green practice. Interviews were conducted face to face and responses were digitally recorded and structured observation of the green initiatives was carried out using the checklist method and supported by a visual aid such as photographs.

2.3. Data analysis

Completed questionnaires were examined, edited and coded, and the data were trans-ferred to an Excel spreadsheet. The data were analyzed by means of the SPSS statistical software package. The techniques used during the data analysis stage of the study included descriptive statistics (such as mean, standard deviation and range) and fre-quency distributions (percentages). The results were presented using tables and figures for ease of understanding.

3. Result and discussion

3.1. General information

The survey was conducted with the owner, marketing managers, general managers and other staff members of 20 hotels in May 2016–April 2017 in India and included both small and large hotels. The considered characteristics within a hotel's profile included the year of establishment, a number of rooms, area (acres), the overall rating on Trip Advisor, price per night and location of the hotel in India. These five attributes were shaped to 20 different hotel profiles, forming the survey choice set as shown in Table 1.

3.2. Respondent designation

The designation of a person in a workplace influences the decisions made by the organization. Owners, general managers, departmental heads and staff members play a key role in the adoption of new strategies for the operation of the organization.

Figure 1 clearly shows that 30% of the respondents were owners of the hotel, 60% were general managers and 10% were other staff members. This means that most of the hotels are run by the General Managers and they are the "Kingpin" of a hotel, very important in influencing and making decisions.

3.3. Drivers for the adoption of best practices for green marketing by hotels

This study investigated drivers for adoption of best practices for green marketing by hotels in India. The respondents were requested to indicate the extent to which identified drivers influenced them in the adoption of best practices in their operations for green marketing. The response was rated in a Likert scale of 5 (where 1 = Strongly Disagree, 2 = Disagree, 3 = Neutral, 4 = agree, 5 = strongly agree).

The frequencies of responses were computed and the results were as illustrated in Figure 2. The findings of the study showed various drivers for the adoption of green practices for green marketing by hotels in India. Most hotels selected for the study are located near the protected areas and in a sensitive environment. These hotels majorly depend on natural resources to remain attractive. Hence, conservation and protection of the environment are important for the continuity and sustainability of their business. Profit increment and gaining a market advantage with rising competition are funda-mental in the hotel industry in India. Thus, practising best practices present an opportunity to achieve green marketing benefits.

Table 1. Brief profile of the hotel selected for the survey.

HOTEL	YEAR OF ESTABLISHMENT	NO. OF ROOMS	AREA	RATING ON TRIP ADVISOR	PRICE PER NIGHT (Average Rates for Standard Room)	LOCATION
HOTEL A	2010	10 tents and 4 Mud huts	N.A.	5	₹ 3000 – ₹ 9000	Uttarakhand
HOTEL B	N.A.	24 rooms (5 standard rooms, 16 deluxe rooms and 3 suites)	N.A.	4	₹ 3530 – ₹ 4621	Rajasthan
HOTEL C	1999	12 rooms categorized as Mela Koth, Imli Serai, Neem Serai and Shisham Serai	35 Acres	4.5	₹ 8986 – ₹ 12,323	Uttar Pradesh
HOTEL D	2006	12 rooms	40 acres	5	₹ 28,883 – ₹ 44,994	Madhya Pradesh
HOTEL E	N.A.	8 Lakeside Pavilions, 6 Villas, 6 Deluxe Rooms	10 Acres	4.5	₹ 2502 – ₹ 7120	Madhya Pradesh
HOTEL F	2008	2 elegant camps of 9 suites each	90 Acres	5	₹ 25,225 – ₹ 45,045	Madhya Pradesh
HOTEL G	N.A.	10 tents and 10 villas	24 acres	4.5	₹ 6483 – ₹ 11,682	Madhya Pradesh
HOTEL H	2010	63 Luxury suites	17 acres	5	₹ 29,068 – ₹ 47,203	Karnataka
HOTEL I	2008	2 rooms, 1 Suite and 2 bungalows	5 acres	4.5	₹ 8682 – ₹ 23,408	Karnataka
HOTEL J	N.A.	80 large aristocratic deluxe and super deluxe rooms	20 acres	4.5	14,277 – ₹ 20,257	Rajasthan
HOTEL K	1997	11 rooms	11 Acres	4	₹ 6500 – ₹ 9500	Maharashtra
HOTEL L	2011	12 elegantly furnished suite rooms	10 acres	4.5	₹ 60,077 – ₹ 64,506	Maharashtra
HOTEL M	N.A.	3 large bedrooms	1 Acres	4.5	₹ 6435 – ₹ 10,103	Tamil Nadu
HOTEL N	N.A.	26 rooms	22 acres	4	₹ 5792 – ₹ 11,390	Madhya Pradesh
HOTEL O	2001	25 rooms	20 acres	5	₹ 37,814 – ₹ 70,675	Rajasthan
HOTEL P	N.A.	12 rooms and 6 family suites, 4 rooms garden facing	6 Acres	4.5	₹ 4695 – ₹ 8746	Uttarakhand
HOTEL Q	N.A.	21 rooms	11.5 acres	4	₹ 6692 – ₹ 29,794	West Bengal
HOTEL R	N.A.	21 AC Luxury Tents	N.A.	4.5	₹ 11,161 – ₹ 11,353	Gujarat
HOTEL S	N.A.	20 rooms	8 acres	4.5	₹ 3594 – ₹ 5584	Assam
HOTEL T	N.A.	16 rooms	17 acres	4	₹ 2572 – ₹ 4437	Uttarakhand

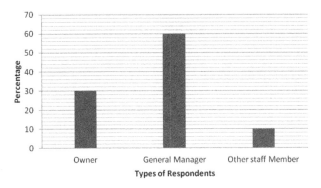

Figure 1. Respondent designation.

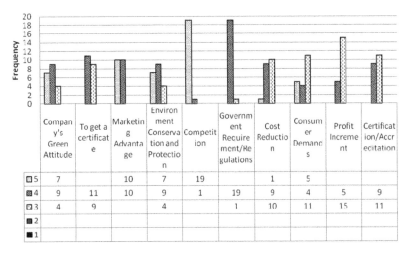

	Compan y's Green Attitude	To get a certificat e	Marketin g Advanta ge	Environ ment Conserva tion and Protectio n	Competit ion	Governm ent Require ment/Re gulations	Cost Reductio n	Consum er Demand s	Profit Increme nt	Certificat ion/Accr editation
▢ 5	7		10	7	19		1	5		
▨ 4	9	11	10	9	1	19	9	4	5	9
▢ 3	4	9		4		1	10	11	15	11
▨ 2										
▩ 1										

Figure 2. Respondent's response regarding drivers for adoption of best practices for green marketing by hotels.

According to the findings, the competition and market strategy toward pro-environment were the major factors which were strongly agreed by respondents for implementing best practices with respect to green marketing. This factor to a large extent drove hotels in India to adopt green marketing. To stay ahead of the competition is a winning strategy. Hotels in India are in competition with other destinations hotels across the globe. They must be proactive in their marketing strategies to continue being attractive to the consumers and fulfil their demands. Secondly, with the growing number of green consumers, it has necessitated the hotels to adapt to green marketing practices to meet the changing needs of consumers and tap the growing niche of green consumers. Thirdly, the hotel business is the highest consumer of natural resources like water and energy. Thus, best practices strategies play a big role in the minds of hoteliers. Some green marketing practices help the hotel in reducing this cost.

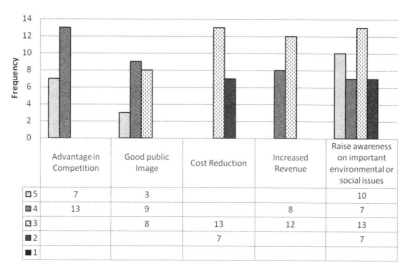

	Advantage in Competition	Good public Image	Cost Reduction	Increased Revenue	Raise awareness on important environmental or social issues
5	7	3			10
4	13	9		8	7
3		8	13	12	13
2			7		7
1					

Figure 3. Respondent's response regarding benefits associated with adoption of best practices for green marketing by hotels.

3.4. Benefits associated with the adoption of best practices for green marketing by hotels

The study further sought to explore benefits associated with the adoption of best practices for green marketing by hotels in India. The response was rated in a Likert scale of 5 (where 1 = Strongly Disagree, 2 = Disagree, 3 = Neutral, 4 = agree, 5 = strongly agree).

The frequencies of responses were computed and the results were illustrated in Figure 3. According to the findings, the major benefits associated with the adoption of best practices for green marketing by hotels are: advantage in competition, good public image and raise awareness on important environmental or social issues. The highest frequency of strongly agree benefit raised awareness on important environmental or social issues. This implies that hotels also understand the need for sustainability in their practice thus promoting awareness of environmental conservation and protection. Hotels have a high running cost and green marketing practices are helping in reducing them to more profitability. For cost reduction and increasing the social benefit to the local area, hotels are giving employment to the local people. More efforts are needed to be put in place by hotels in turning green marketing practices to a competitive gain.

3.5. Challenges associated with the adoption of best practices for green marketing by hotels

The study further sought to explore the challenges associated with the adoption of best practices for green marketing by hotels in India. The response was rated on a Likert scale of 5 (where 1 = Strongly Disagree, 2 = Disagree, 3 = Neutral, 4 = agree, 5 = strongly agree).

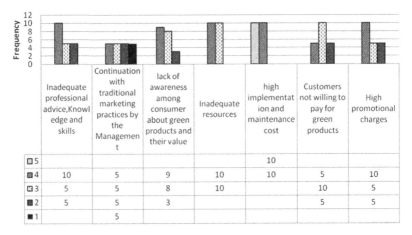

	Inadequate professional advice,Knowledge and skills	Continuation with traditional marketing practices by the Management	lack of awareness among consumer about green products and their value	Inadequate resources	high implementation and maintenance cost	Customers not willing to pay for green products	High promotional charges
☐5					10		
☒4	10	5	9	10	10	5	10
☒3	5	5	8	10		10	5
■2	5	5	3			5	5
■1		5					

Figure 4. Respondent's response regarding challenges associated with adoption of best practices for green marketing by hotels.

The frequencies of responses were computed, and the results were as illustrated in Figure 4. From the analyses of challenges associated with the adoption of best practices for green marketing by hotels, most strongly agreed challenge was high implementation and maintenance cost. This raises a question to whether best practices adopted by hotels in India are really helping in bringing new business. Thus, the cost of green marketing practices is therefore passed on to the consumers who are unwilling to pay the extra cost for a green product that they are using defining the need for awareness among the consumers. Customers being unaware of green marketing products and their uses pass the challenge to hotel stakeholders in convincing the consumers. Green marketing practices are costly to roll out and therefore a hotel needs a substantial initial cost to launch them and subsequently maintenance cost to sustain them. Resources such as time, physical materials, money and skills are needed at every step of the green marketing.

Further, the findings revealed that the most respondents disagreed that they discontinue practising best practices and start following the traditional practices over the years. After entering in the field of green marketing and practising best practices the hotel has already raised their standard and attracted the consumers on that basis. Thus, they must maintain their standard to keep up their record and to have a mark keeping in mind the competition in the hotel industry.

3.6. Best practice of the hotels

All the resorts selected for the survey were located near to the protected area and sensitive environment. According to Rahman (2012), location in a natural setting is one of the driving factors for hotel operators to become competitive in minimizing and eliminating their operation externalities on the environment (Leonard, 2010; Mihalic, 2000). Some of the common key areas of best practices identified were green policy and management, energy management, water management, waste management, sewage

Table 2. Outline of the best practices implemented by the hotels in key areas of operation.

Key areas of Best Practices \ Hotels	A	B	C	D	E	F	G	H	I	J	K	L	M	N	O	P	Q	R	S	T
Environmental parameters																				
Water Management	-	-	-	-	-	-	-	✓	✓	-	-	✓	-	-	✓	-	-	-	-	-
Energy Management	✓	-	✓	✓	-	✓	-	✓	✓	-	-	✓	-	-	✓	-	-	-	-	-
Nature Conservation	✓	✓	✓	✓	✓	✓	✓	✓	✓	-	✓	✓	✓	✓	✓	✓	✓	-	✓	-
Conservation of Flora & Fauna	✓	✓	✓	✓	-	✓	-	✓	✓	-	✓	✓	✓	✓	✓	✓	✓	-	-	-
Solid Waste Management	✓	-	-	✓	-	✓	-	✓	-	-	-	-	-	✓	-	-	-	-	-	-
Environmental Education	✓	-	✓	✓	✓	✓	✓	✓	-	-	✓	✓	✓	✓	✓	✓	✓	-	✓	-
Green Building Design	✓	-	✓	✓	-	✓	-	✓	✓	-	✓	✓	✓	✓	✓	✓	✓	✓	✓	-
Socio-cultural Parameters																				
Cultural Activities	✓	✓	✓	✓	✓	✓	✓	✓	✓	✓	✓	✓	-	-	✓	✓	✓	✓	✓	✓
Contribution to Local Development	✓	✓	✓	✓	✓	✓	✓	✓	✓	✓	✓	✓	✓	✓	✓	✓	✓	✓	✓	✓
Preservation and Protection of Historical-Cultural Heritage	✓	✓	✓	✓	✓	✓	✓	✓	-	✓	-	✓	-	-	✓	✓	✓	-	-	-
Respect for Local Cultures and Communities	✓	✓	✓	✓	✓	✓	✓	✓	✓	✓	✓	✓	✓	✓	✓	✓	✓	✓	✓	✓
Economic parameters																				
Policies and Planning	-	-	-	✓	-	✓	-	✓	-	-	-	-	-	-	✓	-	-	-	-	-
Local purchasing	✓	-	✓	✓	✓	✓	✓	✓	✓	✓	✓	✓	✓	✓	✓	✓	✓	-	✓	-
Staff Training and Local employment	✓	✓	✓	✓	✓	✓	✓	✓	✓	✓	✓	✓	✓	✓	✓	✓	✓	✓	✓	✓
Design and Construction	✓	-	✓	✓	-	✓	-	✓	✓	-	✓	✓	✓	✓	✓	-	✓	-	✓	-
Monitoring and Corrective Actions	-	-	-	-	-	-	-	✓	-	-	-	-	-	-	✓	-	-	-	-	-

management, green education and CSR, nature conservation, daylighting and natural ventilation. Hotel wise best practices of above said key areas are shown in Table 2.

The frequencies of responses were computed and the results were illustrated in Figure 5. The above findings revealed that 75% of the hotels are having a green building design and promote environmental education. But water and waste management are very poor. Socially 100% of the hotels contribute to local development and have respect for local culture and communities. Economically, 80% of the hotels don't have green policies and planning in their system and just haphazardly they are practising the green operations. Even they don't have monitoring and corrective actions system in place. It was great to conclude that 100% of the hotels provide staff training and most of the staff was locally hired.

Energy, water and waste minimization are directly related to cost reduction which benefits the hotel operators. Similarly, energy saving initiatives such as using energy saving equipment, regular maintenance of the air conditioning, per capita green cover within the property, solar energy, using LED and one switch system and proper monitoring of energy consumption were practised. Similarly, water saving initiatives were adopted by all the operators were rainwater harvesting, low flow and dual flush toilets equipment and linen and towels reuse program. In terms of waste management, all the operators were adopting 3R waste management strategy which is recycling, reuse and reduces. The similar waste management initiatives adopted by all the operators were waste separation, composting, purchasing materials in bulk and local purchasing.

Apart from all the similar green initiatives, there are special or best practice initiatives which were conducted by the operators at their own facilities. The best practice was unique and distinct among each other due to policy intention, location, availability

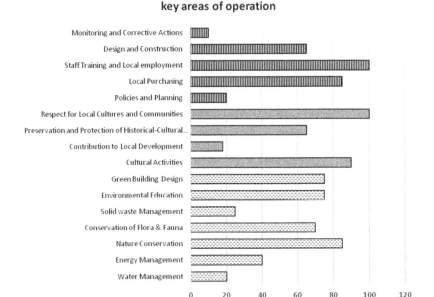

Figure 5. Outline of the best practices implemented by the hotels in key areas of operation.

of resources, and land, climate, design approach and creativity of the operators. Analyses of the unique best practices are described below:

A) Effective Sustainable Management

- **Hotel D, Kanha**—Being a preferred provider of hospitality services, the hotel plays host to several high-profile guests amongst them who's who of India and many high profile international tourists for about 8.5 months in a year. As a result, ensuring safety and security of guests and staff as well as minimizing the impact of the disaster on normal business operations during times of crises assumes a heightened role for the hotel. For this, they have a well-developed crisis management plan.

B) Design and construction of buildings and infrastructure

- **Hotel C, Chambal**—Usage of natural materials for interior and exterior is a positive step toward sustainability and Rooms has been designed in such a way that they are ventilated, aerated and the user can exploit maximum natural light. Construction has been made in such a way that it can easily camouflage with the surrounding. Rooms are constructed using locally available materials. Thatched roofs, local handmade curtains, wooden chairs, tables, doors and other accessories are used in the reception and staying rooms. All the construction is made in local village style and almost all the construction materials made locally and are biodegradable.

C) Maximise social and economic benefits to the local community and minimize negative impacts

- **Hotel J, Ranthambore**—100% of the resort's staffing needs are met by employing local people. They try to improve the skill capacity of the staff through appropriate training programs.
- **Hotel G, Kanha**—The lodge is actively involved in community welfare projects under the support of **The Corbett Foundation** which is owned by the lodge Owner. The lodge has very well recognized the potentials of tribal people from the nearby villages and engaged them in developing hand paintings on the walls of the lodge (with mud and natural vegetable colours). Have souvenir shop on Property offering Wildlife related products and local art. The resort organizes visits to Baiga and Gonds Villages for an educational and uplifting experience. They are the indigenous people of Kanha and have co-existed with the incredible biodiversity of wildlife for thousands of years. They are the true custodians of the jungle.

D) Maximize benefits to cultural and historical heritage and minimize negative impacts

- **Hotel G, Kanha**—A Tribal Museum, established by The Corbett Foundation (TCF), is another step forward in preserving ancient culture. The Tribal Museum features articles made by the Baiga and Gonds tribes. The museum intends to conserve the tribal way of life, their culture, and art. Visitors will learn several interesting facets of tribal lifestyle through illustrative information panels, photographs, and accessories used in their day-to-day life such as pots, utensils, clothes, etc. The museum also incorporates facilities wherein visitors can see artists at work and spend a quiet peaceful night in a tribal hut. The museum is constructed entirely of mud using all local material and runs entirely on solar energy. In addition to the above attractions, Baiga tribal dances, tasting the tribal cuisine and visiting Baiga temple are some of the activities that the tourists can look forward to on their visit to the Tribal Museum. The Museum also houses a curio shop where visitors can buy handicrafts made by the Gonds and Baiga tribes.

E) Maximise benefits to the environment and minimize negative impact

- **Hotel L, Tadoba**—They have installed a sewage treatment plant which is based on the natural method of sewage treatment using constructed wetland. In this technology, called PHYTOROID, the root system of plant species filter (usually planted with *Typha latifolia*) and their natural attenuation processes are combined as a means of water purification. It is one such technology solution which can be easily implemented in the cities as well as in rural areas for treatment of sewage water.
- **Hotel H, Kabini**—They have proper colour coding system in the food waste management (yellow for paper, blue for plastic, green for food waste, red for metal tin/cans, silver for silver foil and white for meat waste). Color-coded (partitioned) bags introduced in Housekeeping for segregating the waste from the

source. Incorporation of trees, shrubs and climber under horticulture uplifted the beauty of the property several times.

- **Hotel I, Bandipur and Hotel H, Kabini**—They use a bio-digester to generate biogas which meets 5% of their cooking fuel requirement.

4. Recommendations

Marketing of green practices practises isn't easy in the short run, however, in long run, it will definitely have a good impact on the hotel and in addition to the clients. Thus, accommodation providers must need to take up green practices that will give cost benefits in the future and drives income in the long haul. Hoteliers can play a vital part in educating the consumers and creating awareness about green practices in light of the fact that the concept of green marketing is new to India. There are some suggestions that organizations can implement to cater to challenges and the successful exploitation of green marketing. It is recommended that the hotel owners and their managers should establish green management policies within their hotels. These green management policies will provide rules, guidelines and prescribe what can be done so as to mitigate the environmental impacts, which radiate from the operations of the hotel. Green management policies will empower hoteliers in a position to draw regulation on set benchmarks for green management execution. The consumer must be made more aware of the merits of green practices. The consumer must be taught and made aware of the natural environmental threats. In addition, steps should be taken to control untrue guarantee and claim by the advertiser to preserve the authenticity and reliability of green practices. For the effective and productive implementation of this concept of green marketing, the government plays a major part of this. The concept cannot be conceptualized unless the government makes specific and rigorous laws and utilizes its authority to be implemented and adopted by the hotels. If the consumer, the organization and the government will work in solidarity toward the common objective of minimizing the unfavourable environmental impact of their activities, then certainly environment can be protected and the world can be made a better place to live in.

5. Conclusion

This study helped to understand the importance of green marketing in the coming years and gives an idea of what factors trigger the hospitality industry to implement green practices in their operations. In the recent times, the image of a company with respect to the environmental sustainability has been of great importance. Although the hotels will take some time to incorporate these concerns into their strategies and concerns. Hotels are a significant component of hospitality industry whose several activities exert a great impact on the global resources. Executing appropriate green practices into their operations will lead to reduced resource consumption and improved quality of the environment. However, it is felt that while implementing green initiatives to minimize the environmental impacts of their operations, there are some challenges faced by hotels. The main challenge is short-term profit and the high cost of investments. Still, there were some common key areas where green management initiatives were implemented by the hotels. These were saving energy, no print policy, saving water, respect to local culture, nature conservation etc. However, the importance of green marketing outweighs its challenges and it's necessary for hotels to be at the forefront to adopt it. Moreover, the hoteliers whose business thrives on natural resources and consumes a lot of water and energy, managers ought to identify what needs to be green in systems, processes and products that will increase business performance in terms of profitability and revenue.

From the results, it can be concluded that customers' changing attitude toward green products and services proved to be the strongest interpreter of implementation of green hotel practices. Consumers are interested in enjoying the beauty of natural resources, so the green marketing is becoming more important for the hotels to attract green consumer 's. Hotels for the consumers demand show that they are also interested in the same and they emphasize the trustworthiness of environmentally friendly products. For this, there is a need for the shift in the consumer's behaviour and attitude toward environment-friendly lifestyle. Then the consumers will be able to pressurize hotels to incorporate green practices in their operations and thus minimize the detrimental environmental impact of their activities. However environmental legislation by the government will necessitate the hospitality industry to adopt and implement green practices at a large scale.

Thus, green marketing is one of an essential tool in influencing consumption patterns toward responsible behaviour in relation to the environment. For achieving greater environmental performance and standards, it requires getting beyond product orientation and labels, and follow best environmental and sustainable practices in their operations. Hotel industry can increase the level of sustainability from the proper building site and design, refurbishing, developing multi-tier green space through selected trees, shrubs and climbers to provide ambience and controlling climate vulnerability like controlling Urban Heat Island Effect (UHIE) and reusing existing buildings, and sustainable construction. Only this way, green marketing can be used as a source of competitive advantage. It was seen that hotels who have implemented green marketing in their operations have an edge in attracting green consumers as well as reducing the running cost in the future. Green marketing should be considered as one more approach to marketing but has to be pursued with much greater vision, as it has an environmental, social and economic dimension to it. To conclude, this study has made an attempt to understand the various drivers behind the adoption of best practices for green marketing. For future research, this study could further be validated in different social and cross-cultural environment. Further, in the current study, only hotels near the protected area were selected keeping in mind the environmental aspect.But for future studies, samples from a different category of hotels and cross-cultural comparison can be included in the model.

Acknowledgments

Authors would like to thank TOFTigers for giving them the opportunity to do the research and providing the necessary support for the completion of the research. We would also like to thank the management of the hotel for their cooperation during the survey process and University School of Environment Management, GGSIP University for conducting the research.

Disclosure statement

No potential conflict of interest was reported by the authors.

ORCID

Chindu Chandran ⓘ http://orcid.org/0000-0002-6349-4365
Prodyut Bhattacharya ⓘ http://orcid.org/0000-0002-4294-5585

References

Barbulescu, A. (2017). Modeling the impact of the human activity, behavior and decisions on the environment. Marketing and green consumer. *Journal of Environmental Management, 204*, 813–844. (Spec. Issue).

Berry, L. L. (1980). Services marketing is different. *Business, 30*(3), 24–29.

Bhaskaran, S., Polonsky, M., Cary, J., & Fernandez, S. (2006). Environmentally sustainable food production and marketing: Opportunity or hype? *British Food Journal, 108*(8), 677–690.

Caputa, W. (2015). Social relations an environmental influence as a determinant of customer capital. *Oeconomia Copernicana, 6*, 109–128.

Chamorro, A., & Bañegil, T. M. (2006). Green marketing philosophy: A study of Spanish firms with ecolabels. *Corporate Social Responsibility and Environmental Management, 13*(1), 11–24.

Chan, E. S. (2008). Barriers to EMS in the hotel industry. *International Journal of Hospitality Management, 27*(2), 187–196.

Chen, Y. S., & Chang, C. H. (2012). Enhance green purchase intentions: The roles of green perceived value, green perceived risk, and green trust. *Management Decision, 50*(3), 502–520.

Dangelico, R. M., & Vocalelli, D. (2017). "Green marketing": An analysis of definitions, strategy steps, and tools through a systematic review of the literature. *Journal of Cleaner Production, 165*, 1263–1279.

Eneizan, B. M., Wahab, K. A., Zainon, M. S., & Obaid, T. F. (2016). Prior research on green marketing and green marketing strategy: critical analysis. *Arabian Journal of Business and Management Review (Oman Chapter), 6*(2), 46–64.

Fukey, L. N., & Issac, S. S. (2014). Connect among green, sustainability and hotel industry: A prospective simulation study. *International Journal of Social, Behavioural, Educational, Economic, and Management Engineering, 8*, 1.

Gao, Y. L., & Mattila, A. S. (2014). Improving consumer satisfaction in green hotels: The roles of perceived warmth, perceived competence, and CSR motive. *International Journal of Hospitality Management, 42*, 20–31.

Geerts, W. (2014). Environmental certification schemes: Hotel managers' views and perceptions. *International Journal of Hospitality Management, 39*, 87–96.

Griffin, J. J., & Prakash, A. (2010). Corporate responsibility initiatives and mechanisms. *Business & Society, 49*(1), 179–184.

Ham, S., & Choi, Y. K. (2012). Effect of cause-related marketing for green practices in the hotel industry. *Journal of Global Scholars of Marketing Science, 22*(3), 249–259.

Jhawar, A., Kohli, G., Li, J., Modiri, N., Mota, V., Nagy, R., & Shum, C. (2012). *Eco-Certification Programs for Hotels in California: Determining Consumer Preferences for Green Hotels.* Retrieved from https://www.ioes.ucla.edu/wp-content/uploads/WDecohotels2012.pdf

Kinoti, M. W. (2011). Green marketing intervention strategies and sustainable development: A conceptual paper. *International Journal of Business and Social Science, 2*(2), 263–273.

Leonard, A. J. (2010). Toward a framework for the components of green lodging. *Journal of Retail & Leisure Property, 9*(3), 211–230.

Leonidou, L. C., Leonidou, C. N., Fotiadis, T. A., & Zeriti, A. (2013). Resources and capabilities as drivers of hotel environmental marketing strategy: Implications for competitive advantage and performance. *Tourism Management, 35*, 94–110.

Li, X., Wang, Y., & Yu, Y. (2015). Present and future hotel website marketing activities: Change propensity analysis. *International Journal of Hospitality Management, 47*, 131–139.

Mensah, I. (2004). *Environmental management practices in US hotels.* (Hotel online Special Report, 1–5). Retrieved from http://www.hotelonline.com/News/PR2004_2nd/May04_EnvironmentalPractices.html .

Mihalic, T. (2000). Environmental management of a tourist destination: A factor of tourism competitiveness. *Tourism Management, 21*, 65–78.

Papadas, K. K., Avlonitis, G. J., & Carrigan, M. (2017). Green marketing orientation: Conceptualization, scale development and validation. *Journal of Business Research, 80*, 236–246.

Rahman, I., Park, J., & Chi, C. G.-Q. (2015). Consequences of "greenwashing": Consumers' reactions to hotels' green initiatives. *International Journal of Contemporary Hospitality Management, 27*(6), 1054–1081.

Rathod, G. T. (2014). Green marketing in India: Emerging opportunities and challenge. *Asian Journal of Management Sciences, 2*(3), 111–115.

Saadatian, O., Haw, L. C., Mat, S. B., & Sopian, K. (2012). Perspective of sustainable development in Malaysia. *International Journal of Energy and Environment, 2*(6), 260–267.

Sert, A. N. (2017). Green marketing practices in hotels: A case study of Doğa Residence Otel. *Journal of Turkish Tourism Reseacrh, 1*(1), 1–20.

Singh, P. B., & Pandey, K. K. (2012). Green marketing: Policies and practices for sustainable development. *Integral Review, 5*(1), 22–30.

Sinnappan, P., & Rahman, A. A. (2011). Antecedents of green purchasing behavior among Malaysian consumers. *International Business Management, 5*(3), 129–139.

Soonthonsmai, V. (2007). Environmental or green marketing as global competitive edge: Concept, synthesis, and implication. *EABR (Business) and ETLC (Teaching) Conference Proceeding*, Venice, Italy.

Swarbrooke, J. (1999). *Sustainable tourism management.* Sheffield: CABI Publishing.

Zeithaml, V. A., Parasuraman, A., & Berry, L. L. (1985). Problems and strategies in services marketing. *The Journal of Marketing*, 33–46.

Zhang, H., & Yang, F. (2016). On the drivers and performance outcomes of green practices adoption: An empirical study in China. *Industrial Management & Data Systems, 116*(9), 2011–2034.

Evaluation of official destination website of Maharashtra state (India) from the customer perspectives

Harshada Rajeev Satghare (iD) and Madhuri Sawant (iD)

ABSTRACT

The article aims to evaluate the official destination website of Maharashtra, the leading tourism state in India, through user judgment approach. After extensive review of literature, the researchers have proposed the instrument to measure the performance of the destination website from customer perspective. The instrument developed, namely "Destination website evaluation scale", measured website on the basis of five critical success factors: quality of information, ease of use, customization and interactivity, identity- and trust-building components and online booking. Reliability and validity tests applied confirmed the usefulness of the instrument. User ratings (collected from 300 respondents) have made the researcher to understand the preferred attributes of the website. Statistical "t test" was used to compare the gap between importance and performance of attributes. The findings revealed that, except the factor "identity- and trust-building components", there is a huge gap (significant difference) between the importance and performance of various website attributes. Therefore, constructive suggestions were given for improvement of the identified critical success factors of website. The findings are helpful for destination marketing organization to acknowledge online information preferences and e-consumer behavior.

从消费者角度评估印度马哈拉施特拉邦官方旅游目的地网站

现今, 官方旅游网站不仅是旅游者的信息门户, 对游客来说也是旅行策划者。印度马哈拉施特拉邦是印度的旅游领先城市, 它在外国入境游客人数中位列第二, 在国内游客人数中位列第六。印度马哈拉施特拉邦有幸拥有数不胜数的游客青睐景点, 其中包括五个世界遗址 (阿旃陀石窟、埃洛拉石窟、象岛石窟、贾特拉帕蒂·希瓦吉终点站以及西高止山脉) 。虽然印度马哈拉施特拉邦是印度的重要旅游城市, 但文献回顾却未曾找到关于旅游网站相关研究领域的可见研究。因此, 此篇论文旨在通过用户判断法来评估印度马哈拉施特拉邦官方旅游网站, 这一方法十分重要, 但在网站评估中用的很少。为了实现上述目标, 研究人员根据从现有工具中确定的网站质量属性/关键成功因素的详尽清单开发了一个工具, 即

"目的地网站评价量表"。这一工具基于五种关键的成功因素来测量网站, 即: 信息质量、易用性、定制&互动、信任&身份建设组件以及线上预订。因此, 这一工具更为详尽, 并且能根据所要测量因素的数量进行更新。再者, 这一工具从客户的角度衡量旅游网站的业绩。详尽的提供了各种属性的选择和释义。经信度和效度检验, 证实了该仪器的实用性。马哈施特拉邦三大举世闻名的世界遗址, 即阿旃陀石窟 (奥兰加巴德)、埃洛拉石窟 (奥兰加巴德) 和象岛石窟 (孟买) 都当选为样本旅游目的地。从每个遗址中有意地选出100名曾访问过该网址的回答问题者组成300名游客的样本规模。这些用户评分促使研究者们了解了网站的偏好属性。"配对测试"用来帮助数据分析了解属性的重要性和性能之间的差异。调查结果显示, 该网站的互动服务和与移动应用程序的链接 (由于缺少链接)的性能评分最低。信任和身份建设组件获得了比其他成分更好的等级 (但远未达到预期)。因而迫切需要马来西亚技术开发公司 (MTDC) 重新考虑网站设计。因此, 应该给与建设性的建议来提升网站的确定性关键成功因素。此项研究结果有助于旅游目的地营销组织了解线上信息偏好和网络消费者行为。

Introduction

Maharashtra state, which came into existence in the year 1960, is one of the most progressive states in India. Along with agriculture, it is known as industrial state, and its capital Mumbai is the economic capital of the country. The state is a leading tourism state of India, which ranked second in foreign tourist arrivals and sixth in domestic tourist arrivals in the country (MoT GoI, 2016). The state is blessed with numerous tourist products, including six world heritage sites (Ajanta cave, Ellora cave, Elephanta caves, Chhatrapati Shivaji Terminus, Victorian Gothic and Art Deco Ensembles of Mumbai, and Western Ghats), 720 km of coastal line, well-known tiger reserves, Lonar crater (third largest crater in the world), and many other cultural and natural tourism products. In this vein, the state tourism policy 2016 of Government of Maharashtra aims to promote the state as "Numero Uno" destination wherein the state will offer vast experiences on global, regional and local best practices and standards.

Maharashtra Tourism Development Corporation (MTDC) is the official destination marketing organization (DMO) for promotion of Maharashtra tourism in the world. Established in the year 1975, the agency is utilizing diverse marketing tools, ranging from traditional media to modern marketing channels like internet. Nevertheless, earlier researches have highlighted the "lack of information availability" and "ineffectiveness of marketing strategies" as the impediments in satisfactory tourism marketing of the state (Joshi, 2014; Thadani & Roy, 2017; *Tourism*, 2014). Therefore, the present research paper aimed to evaluate official destination website (ODW) (www.maharashtratourism.gov.in) which is among very important marketing platforms of MTDC.

To achieve the research goal, the researchers have come up with the instrument, namely "the Destination website evaluation scale". It measured the website performance on the basis of five critical success factors (quality of information, ease of use, customization and interactivity, trust- and identity-building components and online booking) by collecting ratings from website users. Thus, the research study also attempted to provide a standard user-centered scale, in the light of previous studies, to evaluate the destination website. The output of the study successfully provided the insights into online consumer behavior and discussed the suggestions for improvement of the destination website of Maharashtra.

Review of literature

ODW

Tourism is an information-intensive industry where "information" is often called as the "life blood" of the sector (O'Connor, Wang, & Li, 2011), directing consumers during the trip planning. In recent years, internet has become the most prominent source of information among the tourists (Celik & Caylak, 2015; Tanrisevdi & Duran, 2011; UNWTO, 2008). It has dramatically changed the way marketing is done globally by adding real-time responses, diverse array of information distribution channels, viral contents, user-generated contents (UGCs) and so on.

DMOs are the organizations responsible for the marketing of destinations (Elbe, Hallén, & Axelsson Björn, 2009; ETC & UNWTO, 2003; Pike, 2004). Considering the essential role of internet in information search, DMOs turned to online channels to cope with rising new behaviors among users (Ruelnovabos, Matias, & Mena, 2015). Morrison (2013) highlighted that one of the best way to effectively use the internet is through creation of interactive and informative website. Thus, every DMO is struggling to develop an exhaustive destination website.

Law, Qi, and Buhalis (2010) characterized "DMO websites as official tourism websites or destination websites which are created by DMO solely to promote and represent destinations". It helps destinations in achieving DMOs' marketing objectives by improving the destination competitiveness and facilitating the use of destination potentials (Celik & Caylak, 2015; Law et al., 2010). Therefore, website is an essential information distribution channel which plays significant role in destination branding, tourist feedback and market research. Hence not only UNWTO (2008) but tourism researchers have highlighted the requirement and benefits of measuring and evaluating the effectiveness of destination websites. As a result, website evaluation measures have been proposed in many ways and various contexts such as website quality, website performance and website usability over the past duration (Park & Gretzel, 2007).

Evaluation of ODW

Review of literature brings to the notice that Murphy, Forrest, Wotring & Brymer (as cited in Han & Mills, 2006) were among the first researchers to examine online marketing effectiveness inhospitality and tourism, while Ip, Law, & Lee (2011) identified Lu and Yeung as pioneers who proposed a framework for evaluating website performance based on functionality and usability.

Methods suggested by UNWTO (2008) for website evaluation include web analytics and metrics, online survey of users, expert audit and evaluation, laboratory testing and online experiments. These different approaches were used by researchers in different manners.

Qi, Law, and Buhalis (2008) evaluated websites of 31 Chinese DMOs by benchmarking their usability index. Buhalis & Wagner (2013) performed comparative benchmarking analysis to evaluate 30 destination websites with the help of content analysis. A total of 180 factors for each destination website were identified by studying three stages of tour cycle (before, during and after). Fuzzy TOPSIS method was proposed and used by Celika and Caylak (2015) for the evaluation of DMO websites which is based on ICTR model (information, communication, transaction and relationship dimensions). In that method, they emphasize the importance of information, communications, operations, relations and technical performance. Another notable attempt of website evaluation was done by Ruelnovabos et al. (2015), who developed a user-centered standard framework by developing user-perceived quality scale which examines website based on three factors: completeness, usability and influence.

Few researchers have taken a comprehensive review of the previously used methods for website evaluation in the field of tourism and hospitality. Law et al. (2010) summarized the different approaches into the following five types: (1) counting, (2) automated, (3) numerical computation, (4) user judgment and (5) combined methods. The counting method involves counting the number of features and information that a tourism website offers. The automated method uses software applications to record website usage metrics such as page views, clicks and bounce rates. The numerical approach uses formulae or mathematical modeling to measure or predict a website's performance. User judgment deals with soliciting users' feedback and measuring their satisfaction levels with a Likert scale. Last, the combined method uses two or more approaches at once.

Another distinguished review of website evaluation methods was taken by Ip et al. (2011) classified website evaluations methods into two main streams: quantitative and qualitative. Quantitative research usually employs performance indices or scores to represent overall website quality; whereas qualitative research evaluates website quality without the use of numerical scores or indices. Further they described three different types of website evaluation. Here evaluation by phase includes the use of different proposed models such as MICA (Model of Internet Commerce Adoption) or eMICA (extended MICA). Evaluation by features includes evaluation by analyzing contents, design or both. It includes application of content analysis, ICTR model, balanced score card (BSC) or modified BSC, heuristic evaluation techniques and correspondence analysis. According to Han and Mills (2006) and Albadvi and Saddad (2012), content analysis and BSC are actively used approaches by researchers in website evaluation. The third type, i.e. evaluation by features and effectiveness, includes expert evaluation, consumer intention to purchase and revisit.

Thus, though the area of website importance, performance, quality, usability, satisfaction and future prospects is researched by many researchers with multitude of approaches (such as Celik & Caylak, 2015; Law et al., 2010; Kaplanidou & Vogt, 2006; Park & Gretzel, 2007; Romanazzi, Petruzzellis, & Iannuzzi, 2011), researchers admit the fact that the research is still in the early stages of the development as there is no standardized model, dimensions and items for evaluating tourist websites, which makes it necessary to adapt new theories and approaches in terms of measuring and comparing tourism websites worldwide (Buhalis & Wagner, 2013; Han & Mills, 2006; Law et al., 2010; Ruelnovabos et al., 2015). Therein, the literature brings to notice the dearth of research work on evaluation of DMOs' websites.

Besides this, the issue of lack of actual customer evaluations (user judgment) about the ODW is dominantly highlighted by earlier researchers (Tanrisevdi & Duran, 2011).

Park & Gretzel (2007) suggested that website development and evaluation efforts should not only assess the technical quality of the medium but should also include aspects related to customer satisfaction, consumer intentions to purchase, visit or reuse. This will be helpful in improving website quality and developing better customer relationships (Ip et al., 2011). According to UNWTO (2008), online and offline surveys of users measure the consumer satisfaction. As a response, the present research study is a genuine attempt to fill the research gap by investigating the perceptions of tourists about the importance and performance of different contents and design features of destination website of Maharashtra state.

Evaluation of ODW of Maharashtra tourism

The research studies conducted on the marketing strategies of Maharashtra tourism highlighted the weaknesses of lack of visibility in marketing campaign ("Maharashtra Tourism SWOT Analysis, USP & Competitors," 2017). It also lacks in proactive information strategy to attract tourists at decision-making point due to the ignorance toward the study of consumer behavior related to online information search and purchase of products (*Tourism*, 2014).

The present state tourism policy (2016) aims to develop an integrated 360-degree marketing plan including the development of a world-class website for Maharashtra tourism. But the interview of officials conducted by the researchers on 23 February 2016 revealed that till date the effectiveness/success of the website was not evaluated through the online/offline survey of the tourists/users. Further, there was no visible research literature found related to the official tourism website of such crucial tourism state of the country. Thus, the present research is a sincere attempt to fill the research gap by evaluating the website of Maharashtra state from user's perspective which will be helpful in understanding consumer behavior, user satisfaction and perceptions related to the website.

Research methodology

The objective of this research paper is to evaluate the official tourism destination website of Maharashtra state from the perspectives of the users. Primary data have been collected from the tourists (both foreign and domestic tourists) who have visited the website. Three world heritage sites located in the Maharashtra state, namely Ajanta caves (Aurangabad), Ellora caves (Aurangabad) and Elephanta caves (Mumbai), were selected as sample destinations. From each site, 100 respondents who had visited the website were selected purposively, forming a sample size of 300 tourists.

Selection and details of attributes

Having wide-ranging evaluation techniques and website quality attributes, it is almost impossible to establish the standard way to evaluate the quality of destination websites (Park & Gretzel, 2007; Ruelnovabos et al., 2015). In this vein, the first step while developing the tool was to generate an all-inclusive list of critical website features by digging into the main body of the relevant literature (Table 1). These items were later

Table 1. List of attributes and their sources.

Sr. No	Tentative factor	Attributes	Sources
1.	Quality of information	Accurate information, up-to-date information, detailed information on the product, detailed information on the ancillary services, enough audiovisual contents, online booking facilities, privacy and security	Baggio, 2003; Choi et al., 2007; Das & Utkarsh, 2014; Giannopoulos & Mavragani, 2011; Kaplanidou & Vogt, 2006; Luna-nevarez & Hyman, 2012; Park & Gretzel, 2007; Romanazzi et al., 2011; Smith & Ze, 2011; Tanrisevdi & Duran, 2011
2.	Identity- and trust-building components	DMO name, brand logo or taglines, easy URL	Michail & Economides, 2009; UNWTO, 2008
3.	Ease of use	Easy accessibility to the website on internet, easy accessibility to differently-abled persons, easy and fast navigation, easily readable and understandable text, faultless performance, memorable and attractive website design	Baloglu & Pekcan, 2006; Benckendorff & Black, 2000; Das & Utkarsh, 2014; Ip et al., 2011; Kaplanidou & Vogt, 2006; Kim & Shaw, 2003; Luna-nevarez & Hyman, 2012; Michail & Economides, 2009; Park & Gretzel, 2007; Qi et al., 2008; Romanazzi et al., 2011; Tanrisevdi & Duran, 2011; UNWTO, 2008
4.	Customization and interactivity	Multilingual capacity, customization, interactive maps and location identifier, interactive features, interactive communication services, link to mobile apps and link to social media	Baloglu & Pekcan, 2006; Bastida & Huan, 2014; Benckendorff & Black, 2000; Luna-nevarez & Hyman, 2012; Michail & Economides, 2009; Park & Gretzel, 2007; Teerling & Huizingh, 2006; UNWTO, 2008

grouped together tentatively to represent different factors depicting the general website features and functionalities (afterward, confirmatory factor analysis (CFA) technique was applied by the researcher while verifying the instrument which confirmed the segregation with few modifications (Table 2)). Thus, the researchers have attempted to propose the comprehensive tool that uses a combination of attributes identified by prior studies as important attributes for a destination website.

Table 2. Demographic profile of the respondents.

Variable	Percentage of sample
Gender	
Male	72.5
Female	27.5
Age	
1–20	11.6
21–40	59.4
41–60	29
Above 60 years	0
Education	
Postgraduation and above	55.1
Graduation	43.5
Higher secondary	1.4
Secondary	0
Type of tourist	
Foreign tourist	34.8
Domestic tourist	65.2
Duration of internet use for searching travel-related information	
1–10 h/week	30.0
11–20 h/week	46.7
21–30 h/week	13.3
More than 30 h/week	10.0

Quality of information

The quality and quantity of travel information and visuals may affect users' perceptions of destination and can guide him in trip planning (Schmoll cited in Kaplanidou & Vogt, 2006). In this vein, majority of studies used quality of information as a one of the critical factors to assess the website quality (Park & Gretzel, 2007; Tanrisevdi & Duran, 2011). As obtained from previous literature, accuracy, consistency, timeliness, completeness, conciseness, reliability and comprehension are important dimensions of quality of information to keep user satisfied and revisit the website (Choi, Lehto, & Oleary, 2007; Das & Utkarsh, 2014; Smith P & Ze, 2011).

Information also include audiovisual contents such as photos, video and wallpapers which usually represent attractions and places and exert a strong appeal to users to visit the destination (Das & Utkarsh, 2014; Kaplanidou & Vogt, 2006; Romanazzi et al., 2011).

Thus, the factor quality of information deals with accurate information (Cuauhtémoc Luna-nevarez & Hyman, 2012), up-to date information (Giannopoulos & Mavragani, 2011), detailed information about destination (introduction of destination/product, history, location, and features of the products) and ancillary services (like accommodation, transport, guide service and restaurants) (Baggio, 2003), enough audiovisual contents (Baggio, 2003; Kaplanidou & Vogt, 2006) and online booking facility.

Identity- and trust-building components

Considering the failures of the official websites to project trustworthiness, UNWTO (2008) has defined trust as "the user's willingness to risk time, money and personal data on a website". Mentioning name and brand logo on the website separates the website from other websites of similar or "look-alike" names or services. It projects their trustworthiness as an official organization. It is suggested that the official logo should be prominently placed on every page so that users see it whatever their entry page to the site. Further, it is advised that every website should mention their privacy and security policy and mechanism at the bottom of home page (Michail & Economides, 2009).

Therefore, UNWTO (2008) identified these components as "vital confidence builders" for user. Hence, the factor includes the above-mentioned components (Michail & Economides, 2009; UNWTO, 2008).

Ease of use

Ease in using a website makes a tourist to spend more time on the website and access information conveniently (Das & Utkarsh, 2014). The key factor for website evaluation "ease of use" (Romanazzi et al., 2011) is also referred as navigation, usability and accessibility in the literature (Das & Utkarsh, 2014; Park & Gretzel, 2007). Effective navigation is the critical aspect which is usually perceived as the successful movement through a website's pages, including a list of major sections reached easily from the home page and any other page (Kaplanidou & Vogt, 2006). Accessibility means unrestricted access to a website for people and the devices they use (UNWTO, 2008).

In addition, as the markets of people with disabilities and the elderly are growing (Qi et al., 2008), features assisting people with disabilities and the elderly are considered as one of crucial website evaluation criteria (Ip et al., 2011).

Besides the ease of use, website design also plays important role. According to Bastida and Huan (2014), the more attractive and useful an ODW is, the more likelihood to turn a potential tourist into an actual tourist. Here, memorable means the tourist remember the website design on his second visit to the same. Every time user should not feel the website design is new and spend time in searching for the content.

The components such as easy and fast navigation (Baloglu & Pekcan, 2006; Kim & Shaw, 2003; Luna-nevarez & Hyman, 2012; Michail & Economides, 2009; Tanrisevdi & Duran, 2011), easily readable text (Benckendorff & Black, 2000; Kaplanidou & Vogt, 2006), faultless performance (UNWTO, 2008), memorable and attractive design (Kim & Shaw, 2003; UNWTO, 2008), easy accessibility to the website (UNWTO, 2008) and easy accessibility for differently-abled person (UNWTO, 2008) have been included by researchers under the factor "ease of use".

Customization and interactivity

Customization and interactivity are critical aspects of website (UNWTO, 2008). Interactivity is the key to encouraging the flow of information between the organization and the consumer (Sterne cited in Benckendorff & Black, 2000), which has been studied by many tourism researchers as one of the important part of website evaluation procedure (Baloglu & Pekcan, 2006; Luna-nevarez & Hyman, 2012; Michail & Economides, 2009; Tanrisevdi & Duran, 2011).

Website customization is the tailoring of websites to individual customers' preferences (Teerling & Huizingh, 2006). Customization may involve selecting topics of interest, or altering colors or other factors related to the visual design of an interface, selection of language etc. Thus, it includes customization of website contents and design as per preferences and requirements. Research done by Park and Gretzel (2007) highlighted that customization was a factor that was commonly used in non-tourism studies but not at all in tourism-related web evaluation efforts.

Thus, under the factor interactivity and customization, website functionalities such as multilingual capability (Bastida & Huan, 2014; Tanrisevdi & Duran, 2011), customization, interactive maps and location identifiers, other interactive features (tour planner, weather or currency tool, virtual tours etc.), interactive communication services (online feedback, online chat, toll free number etc.), link to mobile application and link to social media pages are analyzed.

Measuring the performance

Here, the proposed scale is based on user judgment that means the ratings are taken from user for each attribute on two 5-point Likert scales – scale of Importance (1, not at all important; 2, somewhat important; 3, important; 4, very important; 5, most important) –and scale of performance (1, poor; 2, fair; 3, good; 4, very good; 5, excellent). Thus, user ratings have made the researcher understand the preferred attributes of websites. This understanding helps researchers to measure the performance gap of website for each attribute. The gap is measured statistically by comparing the difference between the mean value of importance of attribute and mean value of performance of attribute by using paired "t" test. It can be represented graphically with the help of importance performance analysis grid.

Verifying instrument validity

The face validity of the construct was performed with the help of eight experts (researchers from tourism fraternity). They were asked for their opinions on the suitability of the questions. To resolve the ambiguity raised by experts about few sentences and words, some of them were replaced and for few of them explanations were provided. Thus, the face validity of the construct was deemed acceptable.

Further, reliability test and CFA were performed to ensure the reliability and unidimensionality of the scale. Reliability is defined as "the extent to which an individual answers the same question in the same way each time", which is assessed using Cronbach's alpha. Unidimensionality refers to "the extent to which indicators are strongly associated with each other and represent a single construct" (Ruelnovabos et al., 2015).

The pilot survey was performed at one of the sample destination, i.e. at Ajanta caves, Aurangabad, with the sample of 60 respondents. The result of the Cronbach test produced the alpha value of .953 (>.7), which indicates very strong reliability of the scale and confirms that there was no need to remove any item. Next, principal component analysis (PCA) with varimax rotation was done to reaffirm the unidimensionality of the scale. PCA explores the underlying dimensions of each item in order to reduce the number of items into related clusters (Ruelnovabos et al., 2015). Kaiser–Meyer–Olkin (KMO) value exceeding the cutoff value of .50 indicates a desirable sampling (Kaiser as cited in Pan, Zhang, Gursoy, & Lu, 2017). Here, the KMO value was .837, indicating a desirable sampling. The Bartlett's test of sphericity was significant ($p < .001$), indicating sufficient correlations among selected variables.

First, the Kaiser criterion for factor extraction was used. According to the criterion, factors with eigenvalues less than 1.0 are rejected. Based on the analysis, only five factors had eigenvalues greater than 1.0. These factors explained 85.88% of the variance in the data, which is also a good sign. Next, a scree plot was generated and examined. As a rule of thumb, factors to the left of the inflection point or elbow are accepted. In the scree plot, the inflection point was seen on the sixth factor, hence only the first five factors were accepted and retained.

The factor loadings are shown in Table 3. Items F1.1, F1.2, F1.3, F1.4 and F1.5 load significantly on quality of information (Factor 1). Items F1.6 and F1.7 have formed a separate factor which is named as online booking (Factor 5). Rest of the groups remained same. That means Factor 2 is interactivity and customization which comprises multilingual capability, customization, interactive maps and location identifier, interactive features, interactive communication services, link to mobile applications and link to official social media pages. Factor 3, i.e. ease of use which is explained by easy accessibility to the website on internet, easy accessibility to differently-abled persons, easy and fast navigation, easily readable and understandable text, faultless performance and memorable and attractive website design. Factor 4 is identity- and trust-building component, comprising of DMO's name, brand logo or tag line and easy URL. Thus, the scale is now composed of five factors: quality of information, customization and interactivity, ease of use, identity and trust and online booking.

Table 3. Result of factor analysis.

SN	Items	Factor 1 Quality of information	Factor 2 Customization and interactivity	Factor 3 Ease of use	Factor 4 Identity and trust	Factor 5 Online booking
F1.1	Accurate information	.827				
F1.2	Up-to-date information	.829				
F1.3	Detailed information about the product	.874				
F1.4	Detailed information of other services	.837				
F1.5	Enough audiovisual contents	.890				
F1.6	Online booking facility					.576
F1.7	Privacy and security					.795
F2.1	DMO name				834	
F2.2	Brand logo or tag line				.892	
F2.3	Easy URL				.816	
F3.1	Easy accessibility to the website on internet			658		
F3.2	Easy accessibility to differently-abled persons			606		
F3.3	Easy and fast navigation			612		
F3.4	Easily readable and understandable text			.771		
F3.5	Faultless performance			810		
F3.6	Memorable and attractive website design			813		
F4.1	Multilingual capability		705			
F4.2	Customization		.780			
F4.3	Interactive maps and location identifier		.780			
F4.4	Interactive features		.806			
F4.5	Interactive communication services		.590			
F4.6	Link to mobile applications		.800			
F4.7	Link to official social media pages		.764			
	Eigen value	13.480	2.455	1.554	1.220	1.044
	Variance	58.609	10.672	.759	5.306	4.540
	a	.972	.853	.939	.965	.875

Data analysis

MTDC has an integrated website which serves the dual purpose of promoting Maharashtra state as a tourist destination and officially representing MTDC on web. While conducting the survey, the tourists who had visited the website were less in number and hence it was difficult to achieve the target, but after extensive survey, 185 usable questionnaires were found showing a response rate of 62%. Table 3 represents the demographic profile of the respondents. It highlighted that the maximum respondents were male and domestic tourists.

The survey revealed (Table 4) that except the factor identity- and trust-building components, there is a huge gap (significant difference) between the importance and performance of various website attributes. It suggests that MTDC should focus on improvement of quality of information, customization and interactivity, ease of use and online booking facilities, which are critical success factors of the website performance.

Table 4. Result of paired t test.

| Factor | Attributes | Mean values | | |
		Importance	Performance	Significance
Quality of information	Accurate information	3.5072	2.7536	.000
	Up-to-date information	3.3913	2.7246	.000
	Detailed information	3.4348	2.8841	.003
	Detailed information of other services	3.2464	2.7246	.008
	Enough audiovisual contents	3.2319	2.6812	.003
Customization and interactivity	Multilingual capability	3.8986	2.8841	.000
	Customization	3.7391	2.4783	.000
	Interactive maps and location identifier	3.9130	2.5362	.000
	Interactive features	3.9130	2.3333	.000
	Interactive communication services	3.7536	2.3913	.000
	Link to mobile applications	3.9275	2.0725	.000
	Link to official social media pages	3.8261	2.5942	.000
Ease of use	Easy accessibility to the website on internet	3.6812	2.6957	.000
	Easy accessibility to differently-abled persons	3.6087	2.4783	.000
	Easy and fast navigation	3.6087	2.7681	.000
	Easily readable and understandable text	3.6522	2.8696	.000
	Faultless performance	3.5942	2.8116	.000
	Memorable and attractive website design	3.6957	2.8116	.000
Identity- and trust- building components	DMO name	3.1739	2.9275	.107
	Brand logo or tag line	3.2029	3.0000	.218
	Easy URL	3.1884	3.0435	.338
Online booking	Online booking facility	3.7101	2.5362	.000
	Privacy and security	3.6522	2.9565	.000

Conclusion and scope of future research

Official website is a vital promotional tool and important information channel for potential tourist to introduce them to the destination and on which to base their decisions (Fernández-Cavia, Rovira, Díaz-Luque, & Cavaller, 2014). Thus, it is essential to evaluate the website performance. Review of literature revealed that there is miniscule research work done on the online marketing initiative of Indian tourism industry. Adding to the point, there is no visible research done on the evaluation of ODW of Maharashtra state, a leading tourism state in the country. Thus, the researcher has designed an instrument to measure the performance of the website.

The tool developed, namely "the Destination website evaluation scale", is based on exhaustive list of identified quality attributes/critical success factors of the websites from existing tools, and hence it is more comprehensive and updated in terms of the number of attributes measured. The scale measures website on the basis of five critical success factors of website: quality of information, ease of use, customization and interactivity, identity- and trust-building components and online booking. With the use of the proposed instrument, DMOs can get sufficient knowledge of tourist's online information preferences and search behavior which will assist DMOs in improving website design. Additionally, personalized website designs and services can be offered to them.

Users listed customization, interactivity, online booking facilities and ease of use are very important success factors of the destination website. It is followed by quality of information and then identity- and trust-building components. Link to mobile apps, interactive maps and location identifier, interactive services and link to social media pages were considered as highly important features of the destination websites. These features assist tourists in pre-tour and tour phase, making information easily available and accessible. Thus, this study of online consumer behavior advised destination planners and marketers that they should pay due attention on performance of these website attributes to uplift the overall website performance and user satisfaction.

Evaluation of the website of Maharashtra state tourism portrayed disappointing and pitiable picture of underperformance. There is a huge gap between the expected performance and actual performance of the website. Among them, it received lowest performance rating for interactive services and link to mobile app (due to absence of the link). identity- and trust-building components got better ratings (but not as expected) than other components. Thus, there is an urgent need that MTDC should reconsider the website design and improve the performance of above critical success factors to achieve the desired impact of the website. So the website can assist tourists not only in information search but also in tour-planning phase. Providing interactive online tour planner, currency converter and location identifier can help tourists during tour-planning phase while easy accessibility (specifically for differently-abled persons), customization services and multilingual capacity can improve user satisfaction.

Nowadays, majority of tourists search information on mobile so MTDC should focus on optimum utilization of mobile apps and location-based services. Recently, MTDC has launched the mobile app for tourists, but unawareness about the app and absence of direct download link on the website resulted in low download figure and user ratings.

Recent trends of product presentation on the website provided the options of 360-degree views, gamification and virtual tours. It helps the tourists in destination visualization which motivate them for actual visit (Satghare, Sawant, & Ragde, 2017). Therefore, MTDC should take optimum benefits of these technologies.

Further, the website should promote user engagement by utilizing social media such as social networking sites, TripAdvisor and virtual forum so that UGCs could strengthen the online reputation of the destination.

To sum up, there is an urgent need to revamp the destination website of Maharashtra state. Regular online and offline website assessment by users and experts must be performed to maintain the destination competitiveness. Adding to the point, in this rapidly changing technical environment, MTDC should take initiatives for innovative and creative online promotional techniques, so that the ODW will become one-stop-shop for tourists.

The major limitation for the present scale is that it is specially designed to measure the destination website. So in further research, researchers could work on modification of the tool so that it can be adapted to other types of websites specifically pertaining to other relevant sectors of industry. Further research could also focus on performing comparative analysis of destination websites of other states, which will be helpful in obtaining more detailed insights into the research area. Relationship between demographic profile and user ratings can assist website designer in understanding the customer personas.

Disclosure statement

No potential conflict of interest was reported by the authors.

ORCID

Harshada Rajeev Satghare ⓘ http://orcid.org/0000-0002-4321-0919
Madhuri Sawant ⓘ http://orcid.org/0000-0002-6618-8283

References

Albadvi, A., & Saddad, G. (2012). Web site evaluation of Iranian tourism and hospitality organizations: An E- commerce web site features model. *Journal of Hospitality Marketing and Management, 21*(2), 155–183.

Baggio, R. (2003). A websites analysis of European tourism organizations. *Anatolia, 14*(2), 93–106.

Baloglu, S., & Pekcan, Y. A. (2006). The website design and internet site marketing practices of upscale and luxury hotels in Tur key. *Tourism Management, 27*, 171–176.

Bastida, U., & Huan, T. C. (2014). Performance evaluation of tourism websites ' information quality of four global destination brands: Beijing, Hong Kong, Shanghai, and Taipei. *Journal of Business Research, 67*(2), 167–170.

Benckendorff, P. J., & Black, N. L. (2000). Destination marketing on the internet: A case study of Australian authorities. *The Journal of Tourism Studies, 11*(1), 11–21.

Buhalis, D., & Wagner, R. (2013). E-destinations: Global best practice in tourism technologies and applications. In L. Cantoni & Z. Xiang (Eds.), *Information and communication technologies in tourism* (pp. 119–130). Venna: Springer Verlag. doi:10.1007/978-3-642-36309-2_11

Celik, P., & Caylak, M. (2015). The evaluation of effectiveness of online marketing tools DMO's (desitnation management organisation) websites by Fuzzy topsis method. In *Proceedings of The IRES 21st International Conference* (pp. 83–89). Amsterdam, The Netherlands. Retrieved from http://www.worldresearchlibrary.org/up_proc/pdf/120-145146709683-89.pdf

Choi, S., Lehto, X., & Oleary, J. (2007). What does the consumer want from A. *International Journal of Tourism Research, 9*, 59–72.

Das, D., & Utkarsh, G. (2014). Assessing the website effectiveness of top ten tourist attracting nations. *Information Technology & Tourism, 14*, 151–175.

Elbe, J., Hallén, L., & Axelsson, B. (2009). The destination-management organisation and the integrative destination-marketing process. *International Journal of Tourism Research, 11*, 283–296.

ETC & UNWTO. (2003). *NTO marketing activities guidelines for evaluation.* Madrid: UNWTO.

Fernández-Cavia, J., Rovira, C., Díaz-Luque, P., & Cavaller, V. (2014). Web quality index (WQI) for official tourist destination websites. proposal for an assessment system. *Tourism Management Perspectives, 9*(August), 5–13.

Giannopoulos, A. A., & Mavragani, E. P. (2011). Traveling through the web: A first step toward a comparative analysis of European national tourism websites traveling through the web: A first step. *Journal of Hospitality Marketing & Management, 20*(7), 718–739.

Han, J., & Mills, J. E. (2006). Zero acquaintance benchmarking at travel destination websites : What is the first impression that national tourism. *International Journal of Tourism Research, 430*(8), 405–430.

Ip, C., Law, R., & Lee, H. A. (2011). A review of website evaluation studies in the tourism and hospitality fields from 1996 to 2009. *International Journal of Tourism Research, 13*(2011), 234–265.

Joshi, V. M. (2014). Development and marketing of tourism in Maharashtra. *IJMBSPrint InternatIonal Journal of ManageMent & BusIness studIes, 4*(21), 2230–9519. Retrieved from: http://www.ijmbs.com/Vol4.4/spl1/4-Dr-Vandana-M-Joshi.pdf

Kaplanidou, K., & Vogt, C. (2006). A structural analysis of destination travel intentions as a function of web site features. *Journal of Travel Research, 45*(November), 204–216.

Kim, S., & Shaw, T. (2003). Web site design benchmarking within industry groups. *Internet Research, 13*(1), 17–26.

Law, R., Qi, S., & Buhalis, D. (2010). Progress in tourism management : A review of website evaluation in tourism research. *Tourism Management, 31*(3), 297–313.

Luna-Nevarez, C., & Hyman, M. R. (2012). Common practices in destination website design. *Journal of Destination Marketing & Management, 1(2–2)*, 94–106.

Maharashtra Tourism SWOT Analysis, USP & Competitors. (2017, July 4). Retrieved from http://www.mbaskool.com/brandguide/tourism?and?hospitality/3331?maharashtra?tourism.html

Michail, A., & Economides, A. (2009). Evaluating European ministries websites. *International Journal of Public Information Systems, 2009(3)*, 147–177.

Morrison, A. (2013). *Marketing and managing tourism destinations.* New York: Routledge.

MoT, G. (2016). *India Tourism Statistics at a glance 2015. ministry of tourism.* New Delhi: Ministry of Tourism. doi:10.1787/eag-2013-en

O'Connor, P., Wang, Y., & Li, X. (2011). Web 2.0, the Online community and destination marketing. In Y. Wang & A. Pizam (Eds.), *Theories and applications* (pp. 225–243). Wallingford: CABI International.

Pan, L., Zhang, M., Gursoy, D., & Lu, L. (2017). Development and validation of a destination personality scale for mainland Chinese travelers. *Tourism Management, 59*(September), 338–348.

Park, Y., & Gretzel, U. (2007). Success factors for destination marketing website: A qualitative meta - analysis. *Journal of Travel Research, 46(1)*, 46–63.

Pike, S. (2004). *Destination marketing organisations.* London: Elsevier Ltd.

Qi, S., Law, R., & Buhalis, D. (2008). Usability of Chinese destination management organization websites. *Journal of Travel & Tourism Marketing, 25(2)*, 182–198.

Romanazzi, S., Petruzzellis, L., & Iannuzzi, E. (2011). "Click & experience. Just virtually there." The effect of a destination website on tourist choice: Evidence from Italy. *Journal of Hospitality Marketing & Management, 20(7)*, 791–813.

Ruelnovabos, C., Matias, A., & Mena, M. (2015). How good is this destination website : A user-centered evaluation of provincial tourism websites. *Procedia Manufacturing, 3*(2015), 3478–3485.

Satghare, H., Sawant, M., & Ragde, R. (2017). A study of the representation of marketing mix on the official destination website of India. *Journal of Economics and Management Science, 3(1)*, 78–87.

Smith, P., & Ze, Z. (2011). *Marketing communications: Integrating offline with social media* (5th ed.). London: Kogna Page Ltd..

Tanrisevdi, A., & Duran, N. (2011). Comparative evaluation of the official destination websites from the perspective of customers. *Journal of Hospitality Marketing & Management, 20(7)*, 37–41.

Teerling, M. L., & Huizingh, K. (2006). *Exploring the concept of web site customization : Applications and antecedents.* Groninger: University of Groningen. Retrieved from https://pdfs.semanticscholar.org/93ad/dd0956cdcbc5a6f5709e5cdf7f5ea060cb6f.pdf

Thadani, M., & Roy, S. (2017). *India state ranking survey.* Gurugram. Retrieved from http://www.travelbizmonitor.com/ArticleImages/2017/11/30/State Ranking Survey 2017 .pdf

Tourism. (2014). Retrieved from http://planningcommission.gov.in/plans/stateplan/sdr_maha/ch-12-14-02-05.pdf

UNWTO. (2008). *Handbook on E-marketing for tourism destinations.* Madrid: Author.

Consumer engagement in village eco-tourism: A case of the cleanest village in Asia – Mawlynnong

Neeraj Sharma ⓘD and Bijoylaxmi Sarmah ⓘD

ABSTRACT

This study examines the unique role of local community–consumer/customer engagement in influencing consumer/customer satisfaction (reflected in terms of economic activity) and future behavioural intention (reflected in terms of tourism development) in eco-tourism context in Mawlynnong village, Meghalaya,India, which has rightfully earned for itself the title of "Cleanest village in Asia." The study builds on the contents and data from 35 in-depth researches on tourism (in the context of Mawlynnong) with the help of a content analysis (using NVivo 12) method and interaction with 8 local village families followed by structural equation modelling(SEM) analysis (using Adanco 2.0.2). The results show that factors such as cleanliness, local community–consumer/customer engagement, infrastructure, heritage and education enhance perceived trust among tourists, resulting in tourism development and enhanced economic activity by tourists. The participative service innovation behaviour (cleanliness) positively influences exploration intention(tourism) in this context. Furthermore, participative service innovation behaviour (in cleanliness) is found to mediate the relationship between its two driving factors, namely local community engagement and perceived trust in the service provider(tourism). The findings also provide various strategies tourism and hospitality firms and government tourism departments can use to prioritize factors and co-creating a replicable model of service innovation effectively using Mawlynnong example.

客户参与的乡村生态旅游——以亚洲最洁净的村庄莫里农为例

引言: 近些年来,"客户参与"已经发展成为一个重要研究领域,并引起了学术界的关注。营销科学研究所在本世纪第二个十年之初就已经将客户参与作为一项重点研究。认为, 过去五十多年来, 旅游业一直是全球主要的增长型产业。近些年来, 乡村旅游也以可持续发展的旅游方式应对全球变暖和气候变化而备受全球关注。生态旅游通常被认为是可持续旅游的一个次要组成部分, 并且被宣传为自然风光旅游的同义词。生态旅游主要包括: 对生物多样性的保护、对当地居民福利的维持、对学习经验的总结、旅游业和游客的参与、主要面向小型企业、减少不可再生资源的消耗、促进本地人积极参与、为农村人口提供不同所有制和更多的机会。目前, 生态旅游虽然只是一个小产业, 但是在法规和市场力量的影响下正在快速发展。当前, 关于保护自然遗产和自然环境的争论是必要的, 生态旅游在保护自然风景区环境的同时, 也为自然保护区的经济发展提供了一种创新模式。综上所述, 在发展中国家, 开发乡村旅游被看作是可以提高主办国和当地社区的经济地位的有效做法。

研究方法: 本文研究了当地社区在生态旅游中的作用——以印度梅加拉亚邦的莫里农村为对象, 这个村庄有着"亚洲最洁净的村庄"这一称号, 名副其实。本文主要是针对该村开展生态旅游之后影响消费者/客户满意度 (反映在经济活动上) 和未来行为意图 (反映在旅游业发展上) 的因素进行研究。考察的因素包括: 当地社区——消费者/客户参与度、村庄的洁净度、村庄的基础设施、传统遗产传承以及村庄的教育水平, 从而提高客户体验的满意度, 主要体现在旅游业发展和当地经济增长上。本研究以莫里农地区35项旅游深度研究的内容和数据为基础, 采用内容分析法, 与当地8个农户进行互动, 进行结构方程建模 (SEM) 分析。研究内容采用NVivo 12进行含量分析, SEM采用Adanco 2.0.1进行分析。

结论: 结果显示, 洁净、当地社区消费者/客户参与、基础设施、遗产保护以及教育水平等因素提高了游客的感知信任, 促进了旅游业的发展, 增加了游客经济活动。在此背景下, 参与式服务创新行为 (洁净度) 对探索意图 (旅游) 产生了积极影响。此外, 参与式创新行为调节了两个动因之间的关系, 即当地社区参与和对服务提供者的感知信任之间的关系。

讨论: 研究结果为旅游业、酒店管理公司以及政府旅游部门提供了多种策略, 他们可以利用这些策略对其进行排序, 共同有效地利用莫里农的案例创造可复制的服务创新模式。本文对多方关系的研究是独一无二的, 也是史无前例的。因此, 本研究所列出的这些关系对当地社区现有的知识体系、客户参与、服务创新以及生态旅游/家庭寄宿等都做出了重要贡献。

1. Introduction

Over the recent years, "customer engagement" (CE) has evolved into an important area of research and drawing scholarly attention. Marketing Science Institute has highlighted CE as a priority research at the beginning of the current decade. According to Matias, Nijkamp and Neto (2007),

Tourism has been a major growth industry globally for over five decades. Factors underpinning this growth include the growth of incomes and wealth, improvements in transport, changing lifestyles and consumer values, increased leisure time, international openness and globalization, immigration, special events, education, information and communication technologies, destination marketing and promotion, improved general and tourism infrastructure and so on.

In recent years, village tourism has also drawn the attention of the world in the light of sustainable tourism development to combat global warming and climate change (Rahman & Yeasmin, 2014).

Eco-tourism is often considered as a subcomponent of sustainable tourism. Some of the important aspects of eco-tourism are contribution done towards biodiversity conservation, sustenance of the well-being of local populace, inclusion of interpretation/learning experience, involvement of responsible actions from the tourism industry and tourists, delivery primarily to small-scale enterprises, lower consumption of non-renewable resources, mandating participation of locals, extending varied ownership and opportunities for rural people. Governed by regulations and market forces, eco-tourism, though currently a small industry, is witnessing rapid growth as an important constituent of a niche market. In the market, eco-tourism is often advertised as synonymous with nature tourism. Under the current ongoing debated about the necessity to conserve and preserve natural heritage and ambience of natural areas, eco-tourism extends an innovative model for the economic development of such region while maintaining and conserving the natural scenic environment. In the above light, village tourism is assumed to enhance the economic status of the host and local communities in developing countries (Rahman & Yeasmin, 2014).

India had modest 17,000 tourist arrivals with foreign exchange earnings of INR 77 million in 1951. In the course of time, the tourism industry in the country progressed and played a great role in employment creation and revenue generation. After about five decades, with over 3.92 million tourist inflow, the Indian tourism industry earned about INR 50.70 billion in foreign exchange (Gupta, 2007). In terms of expected growth over the long term (10 years), the tourism industry has been ranked fifth. Globally, by 2019, it is expected to be the second-largest employer. The sector was expected to contribute 6.4% of the total employment and generate 40,03,7000 jobs in the country. Indian tourism sector is forecasted to grow annually by 7% over the next decade by the World Travel and Tourism Council (WTTC; Shermin, 2017). The contribution of Indian tourism sector to gross domestic product (GDP) was also estimated to be US $187.3 billion by 2019.

Briones, Yusay and Valdez (2017) have highlighted the importance of community-based tourism programmes for further enhancement towards sustainable tourism development. At an early age, the village children are educated about sanitation to keep the surroundings clean and green (Nagar, 2017). The usage of polythene bags and smoking is a strict no-no with all villagers abiding strictly to these rules. There are heavy penalties in case of any default, which acts as a deterrent. To add on, a complete end-to-end waste management practice makes it sustainable. All the garbage is vermicomposted in the pit, and this organic manure nourishes the green plantation across the village. Planting trees is a part of their lifestyle too. Women have also been considered the causation of environmental nourishment, and a positive correlation exits between women and saving the environment (Pal & Das, 2017).

Mawlynnong is also a model of success showcasing women empowerment through a matriarchal society and a 100% literacy rate. Cleanliness, greenery and warm hospitality to their guests make Mawlynnong an attractive destination for tourists wanting to explore eco-tourism in the region. As compared to agriculture, the income generated from tourism is much higher under the community-based tourism, as awareness and education of the local community makes them capable of extending the best services to tourists and activities to attract tourists (Marbaniang, 2017). The richness of diverse topography, flora, fauna and ethnic groups in North-east India have of late started attracting foreign and domestic tourists alike, and community-based tourism has gained importance (Burman, Cajee, & Laloo, 2007).

A study found that among all lowland rainforests in proximity to the Tropic of Cancer, the region has the highest Shannon's diversity index (Shankar & Tripathi,

2017), reflecting its rich diversity. Some of the attractions/interests for tourists in the region include the presence of "Living Root Bridges" and a naturally balanced boulder on another rock (Kumar, 2014; Nayak & Mishra, 2013). The community work with the earth through the adaption of the living roots of indigenous trees, weaving them into intricate bridges across the ravines. These living root bridges are not only flexible but also able to survive in the flood season which often divide communities (Hroch, 2014). These root bridges are a representation of the ethos of the local populace as being one with nature (George, 2018). These *Ficus elastica* root bridges are considered incredible in multiple technical and biological aspects too (Rao, Bhushan, & You, 2014). Another study found that the majority of the villagers nurture a positive attitude towards tourism as a means for improving their standard of living (Nongkynrih & Das, 2012). Apiculture is also taken as part-time farming in their professions and aids their income from tourism (Marngar & Lyngdoh, 2014). Strawberry cultivation is another such source (Lyngdoh, 2014). Community-based eco-tourism initiatives at Mawlynnong also focus on "organic agriculture" which extends multiple possible engagements in the field of coexistence projects, peace and environmental apprenticeships to tourists, students, volunteers and other interested participants (Baruah, Pudussery, & Universtiy, 2016). Before India's partition, the Border Hat at Mawlynnong was one of the most prosperous areas but later North-east India got virtually land locked due to the loss of connectivity and natural market access of the region through the regulation of national borders.

Conferred with an exceptional distinction of being the cleanest village in Asia, Mawlynnong village is over a century old with an age-old tradition of keeping the surrounding environment clean. The Khasi tribe inhabitants of this village are nature worshippers. There is a village council that has mandates, systematizes and regularly conducts workshops for sensitization and creation of awareness among the villagers about the dangers of global warming. With thousands of tourists visiting from across the country and abroad, Mawlynnong village has also emerged as an eco-tourism destination. The tourism village framework of Mawlynnong acts as a source of economic wealth for several households (Jain & Ratan, 2017). Both the tourism density factor (TDF) and tourism intensity factor (TIF) have witnessed growth in the region over the last few years (Dam, 2017). Mawlynnong has also been as a model of a village enterprise for tourism (Vakkayil, 2017). The success of Mawlynnong has created inspiration for neighbouring villages towards community tourism becoming a movement in the Khasi Hills (Sibi, 2013). There are no resorts or fancy hotels, but a basic guest house and willing community to extend homestay facility take care of tourists' needs (Pathak, 2016). With a sense of firm self-determination, the villagers have been following certain rules as a tradition. Every woman ensures that waster and dust are not thrown and scattered everywhere. The organic waste goes strictly into dustbins, and the collected waste from dustbins is collectively kept in a pit. After transformation into organic manure, it nurtures the green ecosystem of the village. Mawlynnong is an environmentally conscious Khasi community of about all families who take turns in maintaining the roads, weeding, sweeping and cleaning.

Consumer engagement as a concept has its theoretical roots in what Vivek, Beatty and Morgan (2012) refer to as the "expanded domain of relationship marketing." Furthermore, Vargo (2009) refers to this concept as a "transcending view of relationships" from a service-dominant (S-D) logic perspective. This is in contrast to the traditional view of projecting it as a marketing relationships concept under "goods-dominant" (G-D) perspective. Thus, the broader "transcending" relational perspective recognizes that consumer behaviour is driven by the interactive experiences of consumers/customers/stakeholders. These interactive experiences take place in complex environments that also promote co-creation. Thus, in a nutshell, it can be comprehended that specific interactive consumer experiences are the major drivers of consumer engagement. In line with this analysis, Vivek et al. (2012) have propounded within the ambit of the marketing system, consumer engagement as a key concept. On similar grounds, Lusch and Vargo (2010) have suggested that "engagement" can be considered as co-creation of interactive consumer experiences with other stakeholders. CE has been defined by Patterson, Yu and De Ruyter (2006) as "the level of a customer's physical, cognitive and emotional presence in their relationship with a service organization." By contrast, this work attempts to assess, analyse and prioritize some of the key parameters responsible for the success of Mawlynnong emerging as an attractive eco-tourism destination.

The purpose of the this research work is to examine how the heritage of a particular community leads to education, and education results in local community–tourist engagement. Local community–tourist engagement finally results in the cleanliness of the area and better developed infrastructure. In addition to these, the cleanliness of a particular society further motivates tourists and develops a positive behavioural intention to spend more, whereas infrastructure development finally provides the tourists with a sense of satisfaction.

2. Theoretical background and research framework

2.1. CE *in village eco-tourism*

CE has been defined as "customers' behavioral manifestation toward a brand or firm beyond purchase, which results from motivational drivers including: word-of-mouth activity, recommendations, customer-to-customer interactions, blogging, writing reviews, and other similar activities" (The Marketing Science Institute, 2010, p. 4; Van Doorn et al., 2010). Brodie, Hollebeek, Juric and Ilic (2011) also viewed CE as "a psychological state that occurs by virtue of interactive, cocreative customer experiences with a focal agent/object (e.g., a brand) in focal service relationships."

CE has recently emerged as an important topic for marketing studies (Hollebeek, 2011). In case of eco-tourism, an engaged tourist must have a genuine psychological connection with the service besides having behavioural participation. In the extant literature, a few antecedents (involvement, loyalty, interactivity, commitment, trust, brand attachment, etc.; Hollebeek, 2011; Van Doorn et al., 2010) and consequences of CE (involvement, co-created value, trust, satisfaction, commitment, loyalty, reputation, financial outcomes, etc.; Hollebeek, 2011; Van Doorn et al., 2010) have been discussed. However, there is a diversity of views in respect to the conceptualization of the concept. A number of researchers' view CE to be a behavioural construct (i.e. interaction; Verhoef, Reinartz, & Krafft, 2010), whereas others consider CE to be a multidimensional construct including both psychological and behavioural dimensions (Brodie et al., 2011; Vivek et al., 2012).

2.2. Relationship between community culture/heritage and community education

Participation of a community in eco-tourism activities is linked to livelihood generation and other benefits to the community (Tosun, 2005). Local community culture also encourages community learning that results in children learning about the societal value of being clean and keeping the village environment clean for the benefit of the community. Thus, a community gets a sense of ownership, feeling of responsibility and engagement in maintaining an environment eco-friendly, and sustainable can be considered important to policy planners and business practitioners. Therefore, we posit that

H_1: *Community culture/heritage positively influences community education.*

2.3. The relationship between community education and local community–tourist engagement

There is existence of a few conceptualizations about community participation (Tosun, 2005), which are mostly focused on participatory development approaches in development studies through interactive participation of the community members (Tosun, 2005). These studies are mostly based on three typologies of community participation: spontaneous participation, coercive participation and induced participation (Tosun, 2005).

The community members often participate in the decision-making process that may improve the welfare of the local community through providing community education to local community members (Songorwa, 1999). Community participation in developing countries most commonly is used to implement decisions made for tourism development. Community participation in the tourism industry may help in protecting the tourist products and services through community education such as educating community members about cleanliness that leads to tourism development (Tosun, 2005).

In this study, community education improves the local community and tourist engagement towards maintaining eco-tourism in Mawlynnong through the creation of jobs. Since local education on cleanliness helps to bag the village the coveted title as "Asia's cleanest village," this fuels an influx of tourists into the village. The social expectations which are imbibed in the young minds through education transferred to the tourists that further leads to better engagement between the local community and tourist engagement. Hence, we posit that

H_2: *Community education positively influences local community–tourist engagement.*

2.4. The relationship between local community–tourist engagement and cleanliness of the region

CE has been defined as "the intensity of an individual's participation and connection with the organization's offerings and activities initiated by either the customer or the organization" (Vivek et al., 2012). The extant literature includes a number of consequences of CE, such as trust (Casalo, Flavián, & Guinalíu, 2007), empowerment, consumer value (Schau, Muñiz Jr, & Arnould, 2009), satisfaction (Bowden, 2009) and emotional connection/attachment (Chan & Li, 2010). This study offers "cleanliness of a surrounding environment" as a consequence of engagement between local community and tourists.

Community-based tourism has for a longer period been promoted as a development source for the social, environmental and economic needs of local communities. However, this study highlights the relationship between local community–tourist engagement and cleanliness of the region. Since it is noticed that little effort has been made to record, measure or report the benefits accruing to conservation or local communities, this study finds a relationship between the action local tourism–tourist engagement and the cleanliness of the region. Thus, we posit that

H₃: Local community–tourist engagement positively influences the cleanliness of the surrounding environment.

2.5 The relationship between local community–tourist engagement and infrastructure

Infrastructure is defined as the provision of public safety, transportation services, medical systems, financial systems, education systems and other services involved in the population's, as well as in tourists' demand (Crouch & Ritchie, 2005). As a component of the regional tourism product, tourism infrastructure is of special importance for long-term tourism growth and the general progress of tourist destinations in providing the required services to tourists. Despite the fact that a destination has a number of natural beauties, infrastructure can be an obstacle for successful tourism development.

The subject of this work is the assessment of the relationship between local community–tourist engagement and infrastructure, while having in mind that tourism development depends on the relationship between the local community and the tourists for the development of the infrastructure such as road and accommodation as important drivers of improving the tourism sector.

The arrival of tourists enhances the efficiency of human resources at the destination, as tourists require certain services in order to feel better during their stay at the selected tourist destination. In particular, there is an increase in the demand for infrastructure services in terms of water supply, waste disposal, communication and electricity supply as the necessary elements for comfortable functioning of tourists at the selected destination.

Effective engagement between the local community and tourists is important for sustainable eco-tourism. In Mawlynnong, local community mostly depends on tourism as a livelihood option. Hence, infrastructure development is important for the community. Hence, we offer a hypothesis that

H_4: *Local community–tourist engagement positively influences infrastructure.*

2.6 The relationship between cleanliness and behavioural intention (economic)

There is a connection between the cleanliness around the environment and behavioural intention. Tourists intend to spend more if they enjoy the clean and hygienic environment in and around tourist spots. The community contributes time and labour – its investment in the initiative. The time and labour of the community have value, and these are often significant opportunity costs.

It is viewed that the community-based tourism initiatives are mostly community-owned and -managed lodges or homestays, which benefits individual members of the community. Community benefits include creation of assets which are used by the community as a whole, roads, schools and clinics; conservation initiatives with community and collective benefits; joint ventures with community; and so on.

Thus, we posit that

H_5: *Cleanliness positively influences behavioural intention (economic) among the tourists.*

2.7. The relationship between infrastructure and tourist satisfaction

Tourism infrastructure is "the supply chain of transport, social and environmental infrastructure collaborating at a regional level to create an attractive tourism destination" (Tourism & Transport Forum (TTF), 2012). In the literature, tourism infrastructure is classified into four categories, namely (1) physical (hotels, motels, restaurants, transportation, communication and water), (2) cultural (culture, heritage, fairs and festivals, local art and music, dress and dance, language and food), (3) service (banking facilities, travel agencies, insurance agencies and tourist guides), (4) governance (law and order machinery, customs and immigration) and so on. Tourism infrastructure contributes to tourism development that influences the functional complexity and competitiveness (Lovelock & Lovelock, 2013).

The term "satisfaction" has been defined as "the consumer's response to the evaluation of the perceived discrepancy between prior expectations (or some other norm of performance) and the actual performance of the product as perceived after its consumption" (Tse & Wilton, 1988). A customer derives value from their experiences, which enhances their satisfaction (Brakus, Schmitt, & Zarantonello, 2009). Better village infrastructure has a positive impact on the tourists' satisfaction (Figure 1). Therefore, we propose the following hypothesis:

H_6: *Infrastructure positively influences tourist satisfaction.*

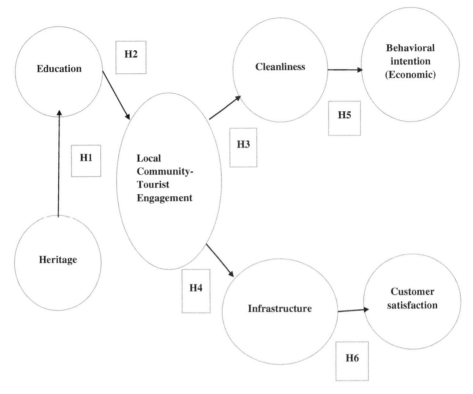

Figure 1. Conceptual model.

3. Methodology

3.1. Data collection

Among other factors, the study targeted examination of local community and CE and future behavioural intention in the context of village eco-tourism in Mawlynnong village. This required that the considered respondents have an experience of having visited Mawlynnong. Thus, the population of interest for the study comprised tourists, local village community members, researchers and academicians who visited or are well aware of the eco-tourism spots in Mawlynnong in Meghalaya.

The efficiency and effectiveness of the findings could be enhanced if studies done by other researchers/experts could provide a firm base for identifying various factors and their mutual relations to be examined in the study. This would help to build up conceptual framework too. Thus, this study adopted a convenience sampling, primarily literature review-based system for data collection concentrated on Mawlynnong. Reputed online databases such as Scopus and EBSCOHOST have referred apart from the reports and articles published online by the tourist visitors to Mawlynnong in reputed websites such as Discovery India. A total of 56 studies on eco-tourism in North-east India were identified. Out of these 56 studies, 21 studies and articles focused on were touching aspects other than Mawlynnong village tourism and were not found suitable for the study. This left 35 studies to be included in this study.

Apart from the above, eight Mawlynnong village residents (representing eight families) having a keen interest in promoting village eco-tourism were also considered as respondents, and a face-to-face interaction during personal visits to the village was done. All the eight family representatives were adults. The villagers belong to the Khasi tribe which is a matriarchal society and out of the eight family representatives, three were females. Although most of the respondents were adults and males, it was males who majorly visited as tourists in groups or as families. Thus, some amount of representativeness exists in the samples considered in this research study. Thus, a total of 35 studies by researchers + 8 village families constituted the sample considered for this study.

3.2. Measurement

The study applied a descriptive cross-sectional content analysis to examine the association between local community–CE, customer experience, satisfaction (tourism) and behavioural intention (Silverman, 2013). The majority of the factors used in the study are adopted from the existing literature and adapted to NVivo 12 Plus software that was used to identify major and relevant themes and codes.

Most qualitative research works have coding, or aggregating material by topic, as a fundamental task. This is not a one-stage process but a cumulative process since the meaning and structure of nodes changes over time. Using NVivo as an apt software for qualitative analysis, the keywords and word frequencies in the context of village eco-tourism in Mawlynnong were done. This enabled identifying patterns across the identified 35 text and responses from the eight village families' representatives as data sources. This helped in finding connections and understanding underlying themes and patterns to enable an informed and supported decision-making regarding factors and conceptualizing a causal framework. A theme node is a collection of references about a specific theme, topic, concept, idea or experience. References to the theme were gathered by "coding" sources at the node. For example, while exploring the data sources, coding of content related to "domestic tourists" engagement practices is done at the node *domestic tourists engagement*. Then, when we open the node domestic tourists' engagement (by double-clicking it in List View), we can see all the references in one place. The major identified themes and codes are listed below in Table 1.

Table 1. The major identified themes and codes.

S. no.	Themes	Mention
1.	Village	216
2.	Traditional	122
3.	Tourist	254
4.	Tourism	563
5.	Sustainable	166
6.	Products	155
7.	Natural	213
8.	Local	247
9.	Indigenous	132
10.	Economic	127
11.	Development	209
12.	Community	313
13.	Areas	140

Based on the codes, the items/factors were clustered by word similarity into the following six clusters:

- Infrastructure
- Local community–CE
- Cleanliness
- Education
- Heritage

The major codes were traced as shown in Table 2 (Figure 2).

The aim of this study was to examine the inter-relationship between the local community and the tourists, satisfaction (tourism) and behavioural outcomes (economic activity) in the

Table 2. Major codes.

S. no.	Node/case	Mention
1.	Village tourism development	32
2.	Village council	15
3.	Cleanliness of village	12
4.	Traditional knowledge	6
5.	Traditional institutions	8
6.	Tourist spot income	9
7.	Tourist sites	11
8.	Tourist attractions	27
9.	Successful village tourist destination	12
10.	International tourists engagement	11
11.	Domestic tourists engagement	11
12.	Village tourism development	12
13.	Village tourism activities	8
14.	Tourism trade	5
15.	Tourism development	9
16.	Tourism assets	10
17.	Sustainable tourism development	56
18.	Responsible tourism	8
19.	Promoting tourism	8
20.	Cultural tourism	7
21.	Community-based tourism	22
22.	Adventure tourism	5
23.	Sustainable livelihoods approach	14
24.	Sustainability	43
25.	Skill production centre	8
26.	Quality tourism products (farm based)	19
27.	Natural settings	61
28.	Natural wonders	6
29.	Natural resources	32
30.	Local community	51
31.	Indigenous people and community involvement	21
32.	Economic benefits	11
33.	Infrastructural development	11
34.	Grass-root community initiatives	19

Table 3. Discriminant validity: heterotrait–monotrait ratio of correlations (HTMT).

Construct	Behavioural intention (economic activity)	Education
Behavioural intention (economic activity)		
Education	0.5264	

Table 4. Discriminant validity: Fornell–Larcker criterion.

Construct	Local community–customer engagement	Education	Customer satisfaction	Behavioural intention (economic activity)	Heritage	Cleanliness	Infrastructure
Infrastructure	0.4988	0.1047	0.7064	0.2223	0.1600	0.5088	
Cleanliness	0.4646	0.3145	0.3072	0.5648	0.2034		
Heritage	0.5526	0.4096	0.2317	0.0582			
Behavioural intention (economic activity)	0.1927	0.2771	0.2074				
Customer satisfaction (tourism)	0.5023	0.1402					
Education	0.2930						
Local community–customer engagement							

Table 5. Effects overview.

Effect	Beta	Indirect effects	Total effect	Cohen's f2
Infrastructure -> customer satisfaction (tourism)	0.8405		0.8405	2.4060
Cleanliness -> behavioural intention (economic activity)	0.7516		0.7516	1.2980
Heritage -> infrastructure		0.2447	0.2447	
Heritage -> cleanliness		0.2361	0.2361	
Heritage -> behavioural intention (economic activity)		0.1775	0.1775	
Heritage -> customer satisfaction (tourism)		0.2056	0.2056	
Heritage -> education	0.6400		0.6400	0.6938
Heritage -> local community–customer engagement		0.3464	0.3464	
Education -> infrastructure		0.3823	0.3823	
Education -> cleanliness		0.3689	0.3689	
Education -> behavioural intention (economic activity)		0.2773	0.2773	
Education -> customer satisfaction (tourism)		03213	0.3213	
Education -> local community–customer engagement	0.5413		0.5413	0.4144
Local community–customer engagement -> infrastructure	0.7062		0.7062	0.9951
Local community–customer engagement -> cleanliness	0.6816		0.6816	0.8678
Local community–customer engagement -> behavioural intention (economic activity)		0.5123	0.5123	
Local community–customer engagement -> customer satisfaction (tourism)		0.5936	0.5936	

Table 6. Construct reliability.

Construct	Dijkstra–Henseler's rho (ρ_A)	Jöreskog's rho (ρ_c)	Cronbach's alpha (α)
Infrastructure	1.0000	0.4669	0.1165
Cleanliness	1.0000	0.6033	0.7020
Heritage	1.0000	0.5746	0.5194
Behavioural intention (economic activity)	1.0000	0.5000	
Customer satisfaction (tourism)	1.0000	0.5396	0.9216
Education	1.0000	0.5000	
Local community–customer engagement	1.0000	0.7563	0.9276

eco-tourism context. The results of the study indicate that traditional and indigenous heritage and education influence CE, which further influences experience, experience leads to customer satisfaction and customer satisfaction finally results in a positive behavioural intention.

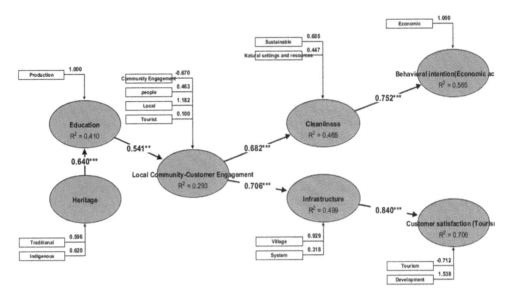

Figure 2. Graphical representation of the SEM model.

The Cronbach's alpha coefficients were calculated and yielded the following significant scores (Tavakol & Dennick, 2011): cleanliness–homestay service quality (0.7020), customer satisfaction–tourism (0.9216) and local community–CE (0.9276). An exploratory factor analysis (EFA) was used to identify the main factors that defined service quality, and variance was explained by the identified factors (Hair, 2010). Finally, a hierarchical regression analysis was applied to examine the relationship between the resulting factors and the dependent variables (Cohen, Cohen, West, & Aiken, 2014).

This study explores the following measures: customer–service provider (community) engagement, cleanliness (infrastructure experience), consumer–customer satisfaction (tourism) and behavioural intention (economic activity). The following scales were referred from the extant literature: CE (Hollebeek, Glynn, & Brodie, 2014), customer satisfaction (Anderson & Sullivan, 1993; Oliver, Rust, & Varki, 1997), customer experience and behavioural intention which was further modified in the context of the eco-tourism.

SEM was used to examine the hypothesized relationships. Using SEM technique, it is possible to simultaneously incorporate the relationships among multiple constructs in a single model (MacKinnon, Lockwood, Hoffman, West, & Sheets, 2002). The overall fit indices of the structural model were found satisfactory (d_G = 2.3631, HI95 = 8.9749, HI99 = 13.3859), heterotrait–monotrait ratio of correlation (HTMT; education (production) – behavioural intention (economic) = 0.5264) suggesting that the model fit the data reasonably well. Please refer Table 3-6 for model fit indices, discriminant validity (HTMT), discriminant validity (Fornell-Larcker criterion), effects overview and construct reliability. A mediation analysis was performed to determine whether tourist/consumer/customer experience mediates the relationship between one predictor variable (local community–CE) and two outcome variables (satisfaction–tourism and behavioural intention–economic) by applying the bootstrap procedure using SEM through ADANCO for performing mediation effect. The results of bootstrap analysis indicated that customer experience partially

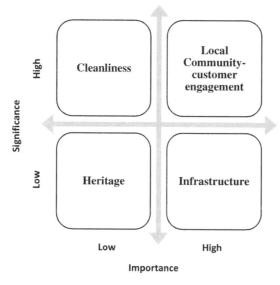

Figure 3. Importance–significance matrix.

mediates between one predictor variable (CE) and two outcome variables (satisfaction and behavioural intention).

Based on the significance and importance of the various factors towards the customer satisfaction experience(tourism) and behavioural intention (economic), the factors are classified as important (on the basis of the value of prediction coefficient) and significant (on the basis of p-value). The one with the highest value is the most important and significant. The importance–significance of the factors is indicated as a 2×2 matrix as shown in Figure 3.

4. Conclusion and discussion

From a theoretical viewpoint, this study extends the existing explanations of the antecedents (e.g. heritage and education) of local community–tourist engagement and its consequences for eco-tourism through a conceptual framework, which finally was validated. This study reveals that heritage (H1) influences education that further influences local community–tourist engagement (H2). Local community–tourist engagement further influences the cleanliness (H3) and infrastructure (H4); cleanliness further results in behavioural intention (economic; H5). Infrastructure finally results in customer satisfaction (H6).

This study suggests that heritage of a community influences education among the community members that further influences local community–tourist engagement. Local community–tourist engagement further influences the cleanliness in the region and improved infrastructure; cleanliness further results in behavioural intention (economic) among tourists, and improved infrastructure finally results in customer satisfaction. In future, the approach/methodology used in this research can consider other service industry contexts, such as hotels, banks, retailing and so on.

Eco-tourism draws a number of tourists in Meghalaya. Eco-tourism initiatives have a lesser requirement in terms of capital and highly educated manpower. This also makes it popular in Meghalaya. It plays a crucial role in developing countries as a source of income generation and contribution to the local community well-being.

The results have established that tourists cooperate with local communities in maintaining cleanliness in Mawlynnong and building local infrastructure indirectly as the revenue earned from the eco-tourism projects are used for village infrastructure development. A major behavioural intention for cleanliness is increase in tourists' inflow to experience the beauty and clean village that give a rise in economic benefit to the local community.

The findings have revealed that tourism businesses need positive tourists–local community engagements in varied areas including educating the tourists the value and importance of keeping the destination clean and building tourists infrastructure. Better infrastructure gives a better experience that finally result in tourists' satisfaction in visiting the place. Thus, local community–tourist engagement helps in achieving sustainable tourism in a region.

5. Limitations and future research

This study has several limitations, which call for further research. They are given below:

First, the antecedents of local community–tourist engagement and its effect on cleanliness and infrastructure have been emphasized in this study. But local community–tourist engagement might also be affected by other factors, such as the perceived cost, perceived benefits, relationship quality trust and various situational factors such as age, degree of socialization and experience. It might be very valuable to study the influence of these factors as moderating variables in different places and groups of tourists in a future study.

Second, although the findings have revealed that tourist–community engagement positively results in economic behavioural intention, more research work is required to analyse and quantify the extent of behavioural intention in adoption of such practices, especially at the household level. This would shed light on how local people could increase their earnings from tourism and subsequently lead to sustainable eco-tourism development.

Third, this study highlights the need for more intensive investment in modernization of infrastructure. Future studies can highlight the psychological and social factors that may result alongside with customer satisfaction.

Finally, this research focused only on local communities in Mawlynnong village, and there is a need to conduct similar studies in various parts of India and in other developing countries. Such studies would provide the basis for comparison and offer grounds for establishing the generality of the findings in the context of a particular country or region.

Disclosure statement

No potential conflict of interest was reported by the authors.

ORCID

Neeraj Sharma (iD) http://orcid.org/0000-0002-1370-4870
Bijoylaxmi Sarmah (iD) http://orcid.org/0000-0001-8272-8385

References

Anderson, E. W., & Sullivan, M. W. (1993). The antecedents and consequences of customer satisfaction for firms. *Marketing Science*, *12*(2), 125–143.

Baruah, J., Pudussery, P., & Universtiy, A. D. B. (2016). Strategy for development and social change in North East India. *Social Action-A Quarterly Review of Social Trends*, *66*(2), 1–20.

Bowden, J. L. H. (2009). The process of customer engagement: A conceptual framework. *Journal of Marketing Theory and Practice*, *17*(1), 63–74.

Brakus, J. J., Schmitt, B. H., & Zarantonello, L. (2009). Brand experience: What is it? How is it measured? Does it affect loyalty? *Journal of Marketing*, *73*(3), 52–68.

Briones, Z. B. H., Yusay, R. M. S., & Valdez, S. (2017). Enhancing community based tourism programs of Gawad Kalinga enchanted farm towards sustainable tourism development. *Journal of Economic Development, Management, IT, Finance, and Marketing*, *9*(1), 51.

Brodie, R. J., Hollebeek, L. D., Juric, B., & Ilic, A. (2011). Customer engagement: Conceptual domain, fundamental propositions, and implications for research. *Journal of Service Research*, *14*, 252–271.

Burman, P. D., Cajee, L., & Laloo, D. D. (2007). Potential for cultural and eco-tourism in North East India: A community-based approach. *WIT Transactions on Ecology and the Environment*, *102*.

Casalo, L. V., Flavián, C., & Guinalíu, M. (2007). The influence of satisfaction, perceived reputation and trust in a consumer's commitment to a website. *Journal of Marketing Communications*, *13*(1), 1–17.

Chan, K. W., & Li, S. Y. (2010). Understanding consumer-to-consumer interactions in virtual communities: The salience of reciprocity. *Journal of Business Research*, *63*(9–10), 1033–1040.

Cohen, P, West, S. G, & Aiken, L. S. (2014). *Applied multiple regression/correlation analysis for the behavioral sciences*. Mahwah, NJ: Psychology Press.

Crouch, G. I., & Ritchie, J. B. (2005). Application of the analytic hierarchy process to tourism choice and decision making: A review and illustration applied to destination competitiveness. *Tourism Analysis*, *10*(1), 17–25.

Dam, S. (2017). Implication of SASEC Tourism initiatives on the North Eastern States of India: A descriptive analysis - SASEC tourism. *Tourism and Opportunities for Economic Development in Asia* (pp. 75-93) doi:10.4018/978-1-5225-2078-8.ch004. Retrieved from www.scopus.com

George, L. (2018). *Mother earth, sister seed: Travels through India's Farmlands*. Gurugram, Haryana: Penguin Random House India Private Limited.

Gupta, R. K. (2007). *Sustainable tourism planning*. New Delhi: Sumit Enterprises.

Hair, J. F., Black, Wc, Babin, Bj, & Anderson, Re (2010). Multivariate data analysis, 7.

Hollebeek, L. (2011). Exploring customer brand engagement: Definition and themes. *Journal of Strategic Marketing*, *19*(7), 555–573.

Hollebeek, L. D., Glynn, M. S., & Brodie, R. J. (2014). Consumer brand engagement in social media: Conceptualization, scale development and validation. *Journal of Interactive Marketing*, *28*(2), 149–165.

Hroch, P. (2014). Sustaining intensities: materialism, feminism and posthumanism meet sustainable design.

Jain, J., & Ratan, A. (2017). Developing a conceptual model to sustain handloom silk industry at Sualkuchi, Assam, India. *European Journal of Sustainable Development*, *6*(3), 413–422.

Kumar, V. (2014). Prospects of cave tourism in Meghalaya. *International Research Journal of Commerce Arts and Science*, *5*(8), 34–43.

Lovelock, B., & Lovelock, K. (2013). *The ethics of tourism: Critical and applied perspectives*. New York: Routledge.

Lusch, R. F., & Vargo, S. L. (2010 September 23). SD logic: Accommodating, integrating, transdisciplinary. *Grand Service Challenge, University of Cambridge*.

Lynch, P., McIntosh, A. J., & Tucker, H. (Eds.). (2009). *Commercial homes in tourism: An international perspective*. London: Routledge.

Lyngdoh, S. (2014). Strawberry cultivation: Horticultural Revolution in Meghalaya with reference to Sohliya and Mawpran villages. *Horticulture, 1*(2), 3.

MacKinnon, D. P., Lockwood, C. M., Hoffman, J. M., West, S. G., & Sheets, V. (2002). A comparison of methods to test mediation and other intervening variable effects. *Psychological Methods, 7*(1), 83.

Marbaniang, I. (2017). *Rural tourism as a tool to empower the community of mawlynnong village, east khasi hill, meghalaya* (Doctoral dissertation). Assam Don Bosco University.

Marketing Science Institute. (2010). *Research priorities*. Boston, MA: Author.

Marngar, D., & Lyngdoh, R. D. (2014). Apiculture: An alternative income generation in Meghalaya. *Indian Journal of Scientific Research and Technology, 2*(5), 90–93.

Matias, A., Nijkamp, P., & Neto, P. (2007). *Advances in modern tourism research*. New York: Physica-Verlag.

Nagar, S. (2017). Innovative minds–Asia's cleanest village Mawlynnong. *Science Reporter, 54* (4), 58–59. http://nopr.niscair.res.in/handle/123456789/40960

Nayak, P., & Mishra, S. (2013). *Problems and prospects of promoting tourism in Meghalaya*. Presented at the National Seminar on 'Promotion of International Tourism Circuits in North East India: Prospects, Priorities and Strategic Options', the Department of Business Administration, Assam University, Silchar, India.

Nongkynrih, D, & Das, D. (2012). Tourism in Meghalaya: A case study of the cleanest village in India. *EXCEL International Journal of Multidisciplinary Management Studies, 2*(12), 65–73.

Oliver, R. L., Rust, R. T., & Varki, S. (1997). Customer delight: Foundations, findings, and managerial insight. *Journal of Retailing, 73*(3), 311–336.

Pal, T., & Das, M. S. (2017). Women and environmental: The analysis of correlation and causation. *International Research Journal of Multidisciplinary Studies, 3*, 8.

Pathak, D. N. K. (2016). Digital detox in India. *International Journal of Research in Humanities & Soc. Sciences, 4*(8), 60–67.

Patterson, P., Yu, T., & De Ruyter, K. (2006, December). Understanding customer engagement in services. In *Advancing theory, maintaining relevance, proceedings of ANZMAC 2006 conference, Brisbane* (pp. 4–6).

Rahman, K. F., & Yeasmin, S. (2014). Village tourism as sustainable development alternative: Empirical evidence from Mawlynnong, the cleanest village in Asia. *ASA University Review, 8*(1).

Rao, B. R. C., Bhushan, P., & You, I. D. A. A. A look at the cloud computing. *RN, 70269, 16*(6), 98.

Schau, H. J., Muñiz, A. M., Jr, & Arnould, E. J. (2009). How brand community practices create value. *Journal of Marketing, 73*(5), 30–51.

Shankar, U., & Tripathi, A. K. (2017). Rainforests north of the Tropic of Cancer: Physiognomy, floristics and diversity in 'lowland rainforests' of Meghalaya, India. *Plant Diversity, 39*(1), 20–36.

Shermin, A. F. (2017). Impacts of rural tourism on architectural and cultural heritage-The cases of Sualkuchi and Mawlynnong, North-East India.

Sibi, P. S. (2013). Indigenous Tourism In Wayanad, Kerala A Study on Perceptions And Sustainable Approaches (Doctoral dissertation).

Silverman, D. (2013). *Doing qualitative research: A practical handbook*. London: SAGE Publications Limited.

Songorwa, A. N. (1999). Community-based wildlife management (CWM) in Tanzania: Are the communities interested? *World Development, 27*(12), 2061–2079.

Tavakol, M., & Dennick, R. (2011). Making sense of Cronbach's alpha. *International Journal of Medical Education, 2*, 53.

Tosun, C. (2005). Stages in the emergence of a participatory tourism development approach in the developing world. *Geoforum, 36*(3), 333–352.

Tourism & Transport Forum (TTF). (2012). Tourism infrastructure policy and priorities. Retrieved from http://www.ttf.org.au/Content/infprio201112.aspx.

Tse, D. K., & Wilton, P. C. (1988). Models of consumer satisfaction formation: An extension. *Journal of Marketing Research*, 204–212.

Vakkayil, J. (2017). Resistance and integration: Working with capitalism at its fringes. *Management, 20*(4), 394–417.

Van Doorn, J., Lemom, K. N., Mittal, V., Nass, S., Pick, D., Pirner, P., & Verhoef, P. C. (2010). Customer engagement behaviour: Theoretical foundations and reserach directions. *Journal of Service Research, 13*, 253–266.

Vargo, S. L. (2009). Toward a transcending conceptualization of relationship: A service-dominant logic perspective. *Journal of Business & Industrial Marketing, 24*(5/6), 373–379.

Verhoef, P. C., Reinartz, W., & Krafft, M. (2010). Customer engagement as a new perspective in customer management. *Journal of Service Research, 13*, 247–252.

Vivek, S. D., Beatty, S. E., & Morgan, R. M. (2012). Customer engagement: Exploring customer relationships beyond purchase. *Journal of Marketing Theory and Practice, 20*(2), 122–146.

Recycling on vacation: Does pro-environmental behavior change when consumers travel?

Jason Oliver ⓘ, Stefanie Benjamin ⓘ and Hillary Leonard ⓘ

ABSTRACT

The existing literature on recycling behavior suggests social and convenience factors are positively associated with recycling behavior. Less is known about how environmental values, environmental self-efficacy, attitudes toward recycling, and attitudes toward recycling effort affect recycling frequency and behavior. Further, recycling behavior is often studied when consumers are at home; behavior may change when consumers are on vacation. Therefore, this article examines understudied attitudinal variables that may be related to recycling behavior using self-report data about recycling from both residents and people on vacation. The study suggests attitudinal variables affect recycling behaviors, and replicates previous findings that people are less likely to recycle when they are on vacation. People who recycle at home may abandon recycling practices on vacation, even if they believe they can make a difference and have strong environment attitudes. The article concludes with suggestions to improve recycling behaviors for consumers when they are at home and when they are tourists.

旅途中的循环利用：在旅行中，消费者平时的环保行为会发生改变吗？

关于循环再利用的现存文献表明：社会因素和便利性因素与循环再利用行为之间呈正相关。然而，这类现存文献对于环境价值、环保的自我效能感以及消费者对于循环再利用和该行为对于回收频次和行为的影响的态度相关研究却较少涉及。进一步说，现存文献的研究对象通常是消费者在家中的循环再利用行为；一旦消费者外出旅行，循环再利用行为或许会发生改变。因此，本文采用自我反馈数据的方式调查居民和外出旅行消费者的循环再利用行为，以探究可能与回收行为有关的态度变化。研究表明，态度变化会对人们的循环再利用行为产生影响，再根据先前的研究结果得出，人们在外出旅行时可能会较少做出循环再利用行为。平时在家会回收垃圾的人，一旦外出旅行，可能就会将回收习惯抛诸脑后，即便他们认为自己可以做到以及抱有强烈的环境态度。本论文于结尾处给出建议以改善消费者（无论是在家的还是外出旅游的）的循环再利用行为。

Introduction

Recycling is an example of pro-environmental consumer behavior (Lee, Kim, Kim, & Choi, 2014; Lee & Park, 2013). It reduces the total amount of waste that is disposed of, and conserves natural resources (Bolaane, 2006). Getting people to recycle frequently and to take advantage of recycling programs for different types of items is important. As noted by Meneses and Palacio (2005), people need to find ways to increase desirable behaviors, like recycling, if we want to solve environmental problems.

Existing research examines determinants of recycling behavior. For example, Hornik, Cherian, Madansky, and Narayana (1995) highlighted support in the literature for the idea that noneconomic external incentives (e.g. actual and perceived social influence) stimulate recycling. They also noted that internal incentives such as satisfaction with conservation and frugality in consumption strongly influence recycling. Howenstine (1993) agreed that consumers must be sufficiently motivated and concerned with meeting social responsibility to recycle. Further, he suggests consumers are motivated by a desire to reduce pollution, avoid waste, conserve energy and improve the future.

For factors that are negatively related to recycling behavior, Hornik et al. (1995) concluded that the basic barriers to recycling behavior are consumer ignorance, misunderstanding, and confusion. They expressed that when recycling is viewed as primitive, time-consuming, and inconvenient, recycling seems improper in a technologically advanced society. Howenstine (1993) also suggested that inconvenience was a main barrier to recycling, noting collection, washing, sorting and storing as obstacles to recycling. The aggravation associated with recycling, along with the required time and effort, may prevent those who do not feel motivated by environmental ideals from recycling. Vining and Ebreo (1990) posited that people who choose not to recycle indicate time constraints, preparation trouble, storage, and transporting the materials are the main deterrents to recycling behavior. Furthermore, Meneses and Palacio (2005) characterize hard-core reluctant consumers, who are less educated, have low positive motivation toward recycling and the environment, and perceive barriers to recycling based on lifestyle and convenience.

The existing literature on recycling behavior highlight social and convenience factors associated with recycling behavior (e.g. Rompf, Kroneberg, & Schlösser, 2017). Less is known about how environmental values, environmental self-efficacy, and attitudes affect recycling frequency and behavior (Schwab, Harton, & Cullum, 2014). Environmental values, environmental self-efficacy, attitudes toward recycling, and attitudes toward recycling effort may also affect knowledge of and attitudes toward recycling policy (Barber, Kim, & Barth, 2014). Further, it is not clear how these factors affect recycling behavior on vacation. The research that indicates people are less likely to recycle on vacation focuses on moral sentiments and social aspects (e.g. Dolnicar & Leisch, 2008).

This research emphasizes other attitudinal drivers of behavior and attempts to address this gap in the literature. The article is structured as follows: 1) Each of these constructs is defined and their relationship to recycling and other pro-environmental actions are hypothesized in six hypotheses. 2) The methodology used to test the hypotheses is described. 3) The results of the study are summarized. 4) The results and their implications are discussed. We start with background on environmental values and environmental self-efficacy and their proposed relationships to recycling behavior.

Environmental values, environmental self-efficacy, and recycling behavior

There is evidence that environmental values can predict the likelihood that consumers will take action to protect the environment (Kaiser, Wolfing, & Fuhrer, 1999; Oliver & Rosen, 2010). Kaiser et al. (1999) illustrated how environmental values and environmental knowledge related to environmental behavior, showing values and knowledge explained 40% of the variance in behavioral intentions. Behavioral intentions explained 75% of the variance in consumer willingness to engage in environmental protection. Lastly, Oliver and Rosen (2010) demonstrated environmental values and environmental self-efficacy were related to consumers' intentions to adopt hybrid automobiles.

Capturing beliefs separately from behaviors is important if you want to understand why attitudes are not consistent with behavior. Therefore, we base our conceptualization of environmental values a conceptualization allows people to vary in the strength of their beliefs, which may or may not drive environmentally sensitive behaviors, including recycling (Banerjee & McKeage, 1994). While beliefs may have changed over time, the instrument captures beliefs along a continuum, so it is still useful in today's market. In general, we expect environmental values to have a positive relationship with both recycling frequency and the number of items recycled on a regular basis (Bratt, Stern, Matthies, & Nenseth, 2015). Because this relationship has previously been explored in the literature, it is not hypothesized in the current paper.

Environmental values develop over time and, thus, are often difficult to change (Burroughs & Rindfleisch, 2002). One reason an individual who is concerned about the environment may choose not to act is if they feel action is not worthwhile or not their responsibilities (Maibach, 1993). This leads to the need to consider a construct which captures the degree to which people feel they can make a difference: environmental self-efficacy.

Environmental self-efficacy relates to the idea that one person can make a difference. Kinnear and his colleagues (1974) called this phenomenon perceived consumer effectiveness (PCE), which they discovered acted as a moderator in the relationship between intentions and behavior. Webster, Jr. (1975) demonstrated that consumers need to go beyond awareness to feel they have the power to make a favorable impact on the environmental problem. Berger and Corbin (1992) and Weiner and Doescher (1991) also provided evidence that perceived consumer effectiveness affects the consumer's likelihood of performing environmentally friendly consumer behaviors. Therefore, we expect environmental self-efficacy to affect the likelihood the customer will recycle and the number of items the customer recycles. As with environmental values, the relationship between self-efficacy and pro-environmental behavior has been explored in the previous literature (Tabernero & Hernández, 2011).

Attitudes toward recycling and perceptions that recycling is worth the effort

Attitude is believed to be an important predictor of behavior (Fishbein & Ajzen, 1975).

De Young (1990) studied attitudes toward recycling in Michigan neighborhoods 20 years ago and noted that the favorable attitudes toward recycling translated into recycling intentions. More recently, Meneses and Palacio (2005) noted that favorable attitudes toward the environment had significant relationships with recycling behaviors. The relationship between ecological concern and the roles that influenced recycling behavior was positive, while ecological concern had a significant, negative relationship with group membership in the recycling rejecter group.

Consumers' decisions to engage in an action like recycling are often a function of their analysis of the costs and benefits associated with the action (Crosby, Gill, & Taylor, 1981). Previous researchers examined the roles of knowledge and perceived value on purchase behavior (Cheng & Wu, 2015; Cheung, Lam, & Lau, 2015). However, less is known about recycling. Meneses and Palacio (2005) demonstrated how this motivational function affects the social role one associates with in the family unit, as it pertains to recycling. In addition to understanding attitudes, it is important to capture perceptions that recycling is worth the effort, which considers this cost/benefit analysis. Both attitudes and perceptions that the recycling activity is worth the effort are expected to be positively related to recycling frequency and the number of different types of items that the consumer recycles.

H_1: a. Environmental values, b. environmental self-efficacy, c. attitudes toward recycling and d. perceptions that recycling is worth the effort are positively related to recycling frequency at home.

H_2: a. Environmental values, b. environmental self-efficacy, c. attitudes toward recycling and d. perceptions that recycling is worth the effort are positively related to amount of waste recycled at home.

Knowledge of environmental policies and attitudes toward environmental responsibility

In general, there is a positive association between knowledge and behavior (e.g. Hoch and Deighton 1989). In the context of pro-environment behavior, knowledge has a positive association with the performance of environmentally friendly acts (e.g. Grunert, 1991). In addition, consumers with higher levels of knowledge may be in a good position to share their knowledge with others, particularly when sharing the knowledge allows them to present themselves to others in a positive way (Kim, 2018).

Attitudes toward environmental responsibility are important in the development of recycling policies and consumer actions. Consumers who feel they are personally responsible and that others should be held accountable are more likely support and adhere to policies regarding recycling. Crosby et al. (1981) reported evidence that consumers from different segments and with varying levels of ecological concern had favorable attitudes toward a policy that would benefit the environment. Understanding these attitudes is also important. We expect the direction of the relationships to be the same as in hypotheses 1 and 2: each of these factors is expected to have a positive relationship with knowledge of local environmental policies and attitudes toward environmental responsibility.

H_3: a. Environmental values, b. environmental self-efficacy, c. attitudes toward recycling and d. perceptions that recycling is worth the effort are positively related to knowledge of environmental policies.

H_4: a. Environmental values, b. environmental self-efficacy, c. attitudes toward recycling and d. perceptions that recycling is worth the effort are positively related to attitudes toward environmentally friendly practices.

Recycling on vacation

Vacation destination stakeholders, particularly those that attract tourists based on natural resources, have expressed a vested interest in tourists' environmental footprint, including their waste management. For example, Cape Cod, Massachusetts tracks waste management as 1 of 15 key indicators that is measured annually as part of their ongoing efforts toward economic, social, and environmental sustainability (keepmassbeautiful.org, 2018). Cape Cod notes that reuse and consumption of post-consumer content decreases dependency on virgin materials, which is important to sustaining the beaches tourists travel to visit. Similarly, Key West, Florida's sustainability efforts include an emphasis on recycling for both locals and tourists. Organizers provide information about how to recycle across multiple touch-points, and make it convenient by promoting a free, "single stream" recycling program that offers curbside pick-up and does not require sorting (www.keysglee.com, 2018). Key West's advertising messages also emphasize protection of the water quality.

In spite of tourist destination efforts to promote environmentally responsible behaviors, research indicates that people are less willing to make an effort to improve the living environment when they are on vacation (Dolnicar & Grün, 2009). Dolnicar and Leisch (2008) compared tourists' pro-environmental behavior on vacation to their vacation at home. Their results indicate consumers are less likely to engage in pro-environmental behavior on vacation. They suggest that people face obstacles to actions that favor the environment when they travel away from home, and that people feel less obligated to behave in an environmentally friendly manner when they are on vacation than when they are at home. This is also reflected in the global market: A survey of 1,185 participants in Pakistan showed that people were more likely to recycle at home than they were in a hotel (Miao & Wei, 2013). Further, among those who recycled, the motivations were quite different when at home than they were on vacation (Miao & Wei, 2013). Similarly, Dolnicar (2010) found that unlike at home, where environmental concern, altruism, and feeling morally obligated are most strongly related to recycling behavior, only income level and moral obligation predict recycling behavior on vacation.

Dolnicar (2010) suggested lack of infrastructure provide was one explanation for lack of pro-environmental behavior. In a different study, some respondents raised concerns about access to pro-environmental programs on vacation (Dolnicar & Grün, 2009). The findings of Imran, Alam, and Beaumont (2014) suggest a similar pattern will emerge. The found that anticipated future use of the resources that were being protected helped motivate stakeholders in Pakistan to behave in an environmentally friendly way. People who live in a place year round may be more likely to recycle than someone visiting the place on vacation because of greater anticipated of future use. Research also suggests vacation time is supposed to be worry-free, selfish time that is free from responsibilities (Dolnicar & Grün, 2009).

Perkins and Brown (2012) linked consumer values with tourism that is related to nature (vs. hedonic). When consumers were more motivated by self-interest (vs. biocentric values), they had less support for environmental conservation. On the other hand, consumers with values that focused their attention on the intrinsic worth of nature were committed to environmental protection, even when they are tourists. There is evidence that pro-environmental behaviors, like recycling, are not as popular when consumers are on vacation (Dolnicar & Grün, 2009; Dolnicar & Leisch, 2008). Less is known about how consumers' environmental values and environmental self-efficacy affect recycling behaviors on vacation.

Thus, to extend these findings, we examine how respondents' environmental values, self-efficacy, attitudes toward recycling, and perceptions that recycling is worth the effort relate to reported recycling frequency on vacation. We expect positive relationships between each of these variables and recycling frequency on vacation (Dolnicar & Leisch, 2008). We also compare recycling frequency at home with recycling frequency on vacation. In accordance with Dolnicar and Grün (2009) and Dolnicar and Leisch (2008), we expect recycling behavior to be more frequent at home than on vacation.

H_5: a. Environmental values, b. environmental self-efficacy, c. attitudes toward recycling and d. perceptions that recycling is worth the effort are positively related to recycling frequency on vacation.

H_6: People are less likely to recycle while on vacation than they are at home.

Methodology

Respondents were recruited from a coastal town in North Carolina, USA. The town is frequented by tourists who typically rent houses on a weekly basis. There are also people who live in the town year round. The respondents were recruited using outreach by a property manager, who sent cards that asked people (residents and tourists) who were in town during on month in 2013 to respond to a survey online. The respondents included a convenience sample of 189 people, which represents over 54% people who were invited to respond, and one person from about 8% of the households the tourism council estimated were occupied at the time of the survey, which includes properties that were not managed by the contact that managed recruitment.

We examine how environmental values, environmental self-efficacy, attitudes toward recycling, perceptions that recycling is worth the effort are associated knowledge of environmental policies at the destination, attitudes toward environmental responsibility, and with recycling behavior at home and on vacation. Existing scales were used to measure these constructs.

Respondents were asked to rate how often they recycle at home on a scale from 1 (Never) to 5 (Always). They were also asked to rate how often they recycle while on vacation on a scale that ranged from 1 (Never) to 5 (Always). They were also asked to indicate the amount of waste they recycle, selecting from the following options: 1 = None – I don't recycle; 2 = I recycle a little – maybe about 10% of the material that would go in my trash can; 3 = I recycle quite a bit – maybe about a quarter (25%) of the material that would go in my trash can; 4 = I recycle a lot – maybe about a third (33%) of the material that would go in my trash can; 5 = I recycle about half of the waste material I generate; 6 = I recycle more than half of the material I generate. They were also asked to indicate whether they recycled each of the following items: cardboard, newspapers, plastic bottles, glass bottles, aluminum cans, motor oil, paints/solvents, and batteries.

We adapted the measures for environmental values and environmental self-efficacy from Oliver and Rosen (2010). We used three items to capture environmental values: *I consider myself and environmentalist; I often worry about the effects of pollution on myself and my family*; and *Environmental issues are very important to me.* These three items loaded on one factor and had a Cronbach's alpha of .760, so they were averaged to create the environmental values measure. Environmental self-efficacy was captured using three items, as well: *It is not beneficial for the individual person to do anything about pollution* (reverse coded); *Since one person cannot have an effect upon pollution and natural resource problems, it doesn't matter what I do* (reverse coded); and *Each person's behavior can have a positive effect on the environment.* The three items loaded on one factor and had a Cronbach's alpha of .776. They were averaged to create the environmental self-efficacy measure.

We also used items to measure perceptions of whether recycling is worth the effort and attitudes toward recycling. Three items were used to capture perceptions regarding whether recycling is worth the effort: *Recycling takes too much energy* (reverse coded); *Recycling only makes sense when it is easy/convenient* (reverse coded); and *It is worthwhile to recycle, even if it takes extra effort.* The three items loaded on one factor and had a Cronbach's alpha of .729, and were averaged to create the measure of whether recycling is worth the effort. Four items were used to capture attitude toward recycling: *Recycling is important; Recycling is an effective way to reduce waste; Recycling is an effective way to help conserve the natural resources*; and *Recycling seems like the right thing to do.* The four items loaded on one factor and had a Cronbach's alpha of 0.965, and were averaged to create the attitude toward recycling measure.

Respondents were asked to rate their perceptions of the importance of having environmental practices in place at the location from 1 (not at all important) to 5 (extremely important). They were to rate their agreement from 1 (strongly disagree) to 5 (strongly agree) with two items: *Tourists have a responsibility to help protect the environment* and _____ *(location) should ban plastic bottles due to the demand they place waste management resources.* Respondents were asked about their familiarity with three environmental practices at the location (banning plastic bags, requiring glass bottle recycling at all restaurants, utilization of a unique glass crusher), using dichotomous (yes/no) responses.

Respondents were asked to note whether the location was their home or if they were there on vacation. If they were on vacation, they were asked where they were staying and whether the location had recycling bins and instructions for how to recycle. (This information was primarily collected for the organization that helped us facilitate data collection, so they could work with landlords and property managers.) People on vacation were also asked whether they recycled and, if not, why not. Finally, respondents were asked to report their demographics (age, gender, household income, highest level of education completed).

Covariates

We control for age, gender, education, and income as covariates. Vining and Ebreo (1990) note age, social class and income are related to recycling behavior. Howenstine (1993) suggests young, better educated, and upper income are more likely to recycle.

We also consider gender because although there are mixed results on the effect of gender (e.g. Martins Gonçalves & Viegas, 2015), Lee (2009), among others, indicates gender can affect pro-environmental behavior.

Results

Recycling at home

To test hypothesis 1, frequency of recycling at home was regressed on environmental values, environmental self-efficacy, attitudes toward recycling and whether recycling is worth the effort. The demographic variables were included as covariates. The overall model was significant ($F_{(8, 178)}$ = 13.19, $p < 0.001$) and the variables explained 37.2% of the variance in recycling frequency. Environmental self-efficacy (t = 2.449, p = 0.015) and perceptions regarding whether recycling is worth the effort (t = 4.038, $p < 0.001$) had significant, positive relationships with respondents' ratings of recycling frequency at home. Environmental values and attitudes toward recycling were not significant ($ps > .10$). None of the demographic covariates were significant.

To test hypothesis 2, amount of waste recycled at home was regressed on environmental values, environmental self-efficacy, attitudes toward recycling and whether recycling is worth the effort. The demographic variables were included as covariates. The overall model was significant ($F_{(8, 178)}$ = 11.552, $p < 0.001$) and the variables explained 34.2% of the variance in recycling frequency. Only perceptions regarding whether recycling is worth the effort (t = 4.122, $p < 0.001$) had a significant, positive relationship with respondents' ratings of the amount they recycle. Environmental values was marginally significant (t = 1.684, p = 0.094), while environmental self-efficacy, attitudes toward recycling, and the demographic covariates were not significant ($ps > 0.10$).

Hypothesis 2 was also tested using the number of items recycled as the dependent variable. Table 1 indicates what people noted they recycle and shows the percentage of respondents by the number of items they recycle from the list. The number of items they recycle was calculated by adding the items they recycled (cardboard, newspapers, plastic bottles, glass bottles, aluminum cans, motor oil, paints/solvents, and batteries).

The number of items recycled was the dependent variable. The items recycled variable was regressed on environmental values, environmental self-efficacy, attitudes toward recycling and whether recycling is worth the effort. The demographic variables were included as covariates. Environmental self-efficacy (t = 2.274, p = 0.024) and perceptions that recycling is worth the effort (t = 3.669, $p < 0.001$) had significant, positive associations with the

Table 1. What people in the sample recycle.

Item	Number	% of Sample
Plastic bottles	174	87
Cardboard	173	86.5
Aluminum cans	172	86
Glass bottles	166	83
Newspapers	160	80
Batteries	74	37
Motor oil	53	26.5
Paints and solvents	51	25.5
Don't recycle	14	7

number of different items recycled. Environmental values, attitude toward recycling, age, gender, education, income and whether they were locals/visitors did not have significant relationships (ps> 0.10) with the number of items they recycle on an ongoing basis. The equation explained 35% of the variance in the number of items recycled.

Knowledge of environmentally friendly practices

Hypothesis 3 suggested environmental values, environmental self-efficacy, attitudes toward recycling, and perceptions that recycling is worth the effort would predict consumer familiarity with environmental policies. Dichotomous variables that captured knowledge of three environmental policies were used as dependent variables: some stores at the location banned plastic bags, the location required recycling of glass bottles at restaurants, and the utilization of a unique glass recycling crusher. The independent variables included environmental values, environmental self-efficacy, attitude toward recycling, and perceptions of whether recycling is worth the effort.

The demographic variables and whether the respondent was a resident or a visitor were included as covariates. Gender and residency were coded as categorical variables. Table 2 shows the results of the logistic regressions on each of these dependent variables. Generally, residency at the location had the greatest influence on knowledge of the local environmental practices. Perceptions that recycling is worth the effort was a significant predictor of knowledge of one of the three policies. The analysis was repeated with only the residents included, but did not yield significant chi-squares from any of the analyses. Therefore, hypothesis 3 was not supported by the results.

Attitudes toward environmentally friendly practices

To test hypothesis 4, three separate regressions were run. First, the perceived importance of environmental practices at the location was regressed on environmental values, environmental self-efficacy, attitudes toward recycling and whether recycling is worth the effort. The demographic variables and residency at the location were included as covariates. The overall model was significant ($F (9, 177) = 35.415$, $p< 0.001$) and the variables explained 64.3% of the variance in recycling frequency. Environmental self-efficacy ($t = 4.500$, $p< .001$), attitudes toward recycling ($t = 7.225$, $p< 0.001$) and gender ($t = 2.186$, $p< 0.001$, suggesting females gave higher ratings) had significant, positive

Table 2. Knowledge of Environmental Policies.

	Plastic Bags		Glass Bottles		Glass Crusher	
	β	Sig.	β	Sig.	β	Sig.
Environmental values	0.483	> 0.10	0.381	> 0.10	−0.098	> 0.10
Environmental self-efficacy	−0.794	> 0.10	−0.227	> 0.10	−0.590	> 0.10
Attitude toward recycling	0.413	> 0.10	−0.050	> 0.10	0.098	> 0.10
Recycling worth effort	−0.266	> 0.10	−0.068	> 0.10	0.734	0.028
Age	−0.155	> 0.10	0.134	> 0.10	−0.121	> 0.10
Gender	−0.640	> 0.10	−0.828	0.062	−0.173	> 0.10
Education	−0.138	> 0.10	−0.134	> 0.10	−0.022	> 0.10
Income	−0.088	> 0.10	0.092	> 0.10	−0.089	> 0.10
Resident (0 = Resident, 1 = Visitor)	−3.068	< 0.001	−2.685	< 0.001	−2.939	< 0.001
Percentage correct	89.3%		80.2%		78.1%	
Nagelkerke R^2	0.368		0.420		0.408	

relationships with the perceived importance of environmental practices at the location. Environmental values, whether recycling effort is worthwhile, residency and the other demographic covariates were not significant (ps> 0.10).

Next, tourist responsibility for upholding environmental practices was regressed on environmental values, environmental self-efficacy, attitudes toward recycling and whether recycling is worth the effort. The demographic variables and residency at the location were included as covariates. The overall model was significant (F (9, 177) = 15.737, p< 0.001) and the variables explained 44.5% of the variance in tourist responsibility. Environmental self-efficacy (t = 2.658, p = 0.009) and attitudes toward recycling (t = 5.266, p< 0.001) had significant, positive relationships with the tourist responsibility at the location. Environmental values, whether recycling effort is worthwhile, residency and the demographic covariates were not significant (ps>0.10).

Finally, agreement with whether plastic bottles should be banned from the location was regressed on environmental values, environmental self-efficacy, attitudes toward recycling and whether recycling is worth the effort. Once again, the demographic variables and residency at the location were included as covariates. The overall model was significant (F (9, 177) = 5.376, p< 0.001) and the variables explained 21.5% of the variance in recycling frequency. Environmental values (t = 2.570, p = 0.011) and attitudes toward recycling (t = 2.070, p = 0.040) had significant, positive relationships with the tourist responsibility at the location. Environmental self-efficacy, whether recycling effort is worthwhile, residency and the demographic covariates were not significant (ps> 0.10).

Recycling on vacation

To test hypothesis 5, the frequency of recycling on vacation was regressed on environmental values, environmental self-efficacy, attitudes toward recycling and whether recycling is worth the effort. The demographic variables were included as covariates. The overall model was significant (F (8, 178) = 12.467, p< 0.001) and the variables explained 35.9% of the variance in recycling frequency. Environmental values (t = 3.455, p = 0.001) and perceptions that recycling is worth the effort (t = 3.863, p< 0.001) had significant, positive relationships with recycling frequency on vacation. Environmental self-efficacy, attitude toward recycling, and the demographic covariates were not significant (ps> 0.10).

Hypothesis 6 suggested respondents were less likely to recycle on vacation than they were at home. Respondents' ratings of how often they recycle at home and, separately, while on vacation on a scale that ranged from 1 (Never) to 5 (Always) were compared. Table 3 provides a frequency of each response. The frequencies indicate the number of people who always recycle at home far exceeds the number of

Table 3. In general, how often do you recycle....

	At Home		On Vacation	
	Frequency	Percent	Frequency	Percent
Always	144	72	49	24.5
Usually	23	11.5	55	27.5
About Half the Time	7	3.5	26	13
Rarely	11	7	44	22
Never	14	7	25	12.5

people who always recycle on vacation. To examine the statistical significance of this relationship, we conducted a repeated measures analysis with two levels: at home and on vacation.

The initial analysis compared the two ratings and indicates there is a significant difference between the regularity of recycling on vacation vs. at home (Wilks' Lambda = 0.571; $F(1, 198) = 148.97$, p< 0.001). Respondents were significantly more likely to recycle at home (M = 4.367) than they were to recycle while on vacation (M = 3.296).

When environmental values, environmental self-efficacy, attitude toward recycling, and perceptions of whether recycling is worth the effort are included in the analysis as covariates, being at home still has a significant, positive effect on recycling frequency (Wilks' Lambda = 0.979, p< 0.05; M_{home} = 4.417 vs. $M_{vacation}$ = 3.342), and interacts with environmental values (Wilks' Lambda = 0.946, p = 0.002) and attitudes toward recycling (Wilks' Lambda = 0.978, p – 0.045). Both environmental values and attitudes toward recycling increased the likelihood that the respondent recycled on vacation. In the test of between-subjects effects, environmental values ($F(1, 182) = 6.859$, p = 0.01); environmental self-efficacy ($F(1, 182) = 4.985$, p = 0.027); and perceptions that recycling is worth the effort ($F(1, 182) = 22.57$, p< 0.001) had significant, positive relationships with the average frequency of recycling behavior, with the transformed average of recycling frequency at home and on vacation as the dependent variable.

As a post hoc analysis, we did an exploratory examination of the people who reported they were on vacation at the location. We identified the 27 respondents who noted they did not recycle while on vacation and categorized their reasons why not. The most common response was a lack of knowledge about how or where to recycle (67% of respondents who did not recycle). Other barriers included forgetting (15%), perception it was too messy (7%), perception it was a hassle (7%), and lack of time to sort and bundle items (4%).

Discussion

In this study of how environmental values, attitudes towards recycling, perceptions of the value of recycling and environmental self-efficacy predict recycling behaviors, attitudes, and knowledge, we found that that the pattern of predictors varied based on the outcome including if the behavior was at home or on vacation.

When looking at recycling behavior at home, we found that beliefs that one person can make an impact on the environment and that attitudes that recycling efforts are worthwhile explain a substantial amount (35–37%) of the variance related to recycling frequency and items recycled. This is in line with previous research that demonstrates that self-efficacy increases pro environmental behaviors specifically recycling (Tabernero & Hernández, 2011). However, when looking at recycling behavior while on vacation, self-efficacy does not explain recycling behavior. Instead, belief that recycling efforts are worthwhile and environmental values accounts for 36% of the variability in recycling frequency while on vacation. This difference in accounting for recycling frequency at home versus while on vacation indicates different factors at play and the need for different interventions to might be appropriate to encourage recycling behavior of vacationers.

Our findings on attitudes towards environmental practices and policies, knowledge of local environmental policies offer additional insight into recycling at home and on vacation. Attitude towards recycling was positively associated with support for a plastic bottle ban, belief that tourists are responsible for upholding environmental practices and that environmental practices are important at the location. This indicates that positive attitude towards one particular environmental practice (recycling) predicts support for other related environmental practices (plastic bottle ban) and general support for environmental practices. The belief that one's actions have an impact on the environment (self-efficacy) explains attitudes toward the importance of local environmental practices and tourist responsibility for upholding those environmental behaviors. This suggests that beliefs that one can have an impact relates to the importance of those behaviors whereas support for a plastic bottle ban, which is not related to an individual behavior, is not predicted by self-efficacy.

This study demonstrates a new finding that recycling behavior varies at home and while on vacation with individuals recycling less on vacation. Further, frequency of recycling is explained by different factors when at home versus while on vacation. Frequency of recycling on vacation, unlike while at home, is explained by environmental values but not self-efficacy. Prior research indicates that barriers to recycling and choices not to recycle relate to issues of convenience, messinesss, and knowledge (Hornik et al., 1995; Vining & Ebreo, 1990), the same dimensions uncovered as issues in our analysis of individual explanations for why they did not recycle on vacation. Thus while on vacation, a tourist may be less likely to feel the ability to have an effect on the environment or may simply less goal oriented or motivated. Town managers and policy makers could endeavor to make recycling as compatible with vacation behaviors as possible by making it fun or relaxing so it is seen as different from the day to day industrious tasks one may try to escape on vacation.

The current study is limited to a convenience sample from one market. Future research should replicate the results with a representative sample and in different markets before generalizing the results. It can examine differences between tourists who revisit the same location and first time visitors, as they are likely to differ in their anticipated future use of the destination. It can also examine the effects of priming tourists to think about their environmental values, which has had positive effects on pro-environmental behaviors in other contexts.

Hornik et al. (1995) recommended increasing recycling education and improve the social image of recycling activities to promote recycling at home. They suggest policy makers highlight the importance and availability of recycling, or how to recycle quickly and conveniently. They also suggest that the social influence of neighbors, friends, and family members can extend the recycling behaviors, which is consistent with Kim (2018). Similar efforts may promote recycling among consumers on vacation. We also echo past advice that suggests it is important to emphasize the collective importance of recycling (Meneses & Palacio, 2005). However, the current studies indicate it is also important to communicate that the individual consumer can make a difference.

Environmental self-efficacy was a significant predictor of recycling frequency at home and the number of different items recycled. It was also a significant predictor of perceptions that environmental policies and tourist recycling efforts were important. Therefore, education should go beyond the role of an individual as a member of society to emphasize the importance of contributions the individual can make on his/her own. Doing so would remind consumers with high self-efficacy that they can make a difference. In the same way, if a consumer feels the recycling process is important, recent communication interventions suggest that among highly motivated consumers, using cuteness as a communication intervention can impact recycling behavior (Wang, Mukhopadhyay, & Patrick, 2017). Communications that target segments that need to be reminded or need a nudge can be implemented in tourist areas to increase the likelihood that consumers who recycle at home do so on vacation.

Disclosure statement

No potential conflict of interest was reported by the authors.

ORCID

Jason Oliver ⓘ http://orcid.org/0000-0002-2203-6595
Stefanie Benjamin ⓘ http://orcid.org/0000-0002-4653-6754
Hillary Leonard ⓘ http://orcid.org/0000-0003-4764-8405

References

Banerjee, S. B., & McKeage, K. (1994). How green is my value? Exploring the relationship between environmentalism and materialism. In C. Allen & D. Roedder John (Eds.), *Advances in consumer research* (Vol. 21, pp. 147–152). Provo, UT: Association for Consumer Research. http://acrwebsite.org/volumes/7575/volumes/v21/NA-21

Barber, N. A., Kim, Y. H., & Barth, S. (2014). The importance of recycling to US festival visitors: A preliminary study. *Journal of Hospitality Marketing & Management, 23*(6), 601–625.

Berger, I. E., & Corbin, R. M. (1992). Perceived consumer effectiveness and faith in others as moderators of environmentally responsible behaviors. *Journal of Public Policy and Marketing, 11*, 79–89.

Bolaane, B. (2006). Constraints to promoting people centered approaches in recycling. *Habitat International, 30*(4), 731.

Bratt, C., Stern, P. C., Matthies, E., & Nenseth, V. (2015). Home, car use, and vacation: The structure of environmentally significant individual behavior. *Environment and Behavior, 47*(4), 436–473.

Burroughs, J. E., & Rindfleisch, A. (2002). Materialism and well-being: A conflicting values perspective. *Journal of Consumer Research, 29*(3), 348–363.

Cheng, T. M., & Wu, H. C. (2015). How do environmental knowledge, environmental sensitivity, and place attachment affect environmentally responsible behavior? An integrated approach for sustainable island tourism. *Journal of Sustainable Tourism, 23*(4), 557–576.

Cheung, R., Lam, A. Y., & Lau, M. M. (2015). Drivers of green product adoption: The role of green perceived value, green trust and perceived quality. *Journal of Global Scholars of Marketing Science, 25*(3), 232–245.

Crosby, L., Gill, J., & Taylor, J. (1981). Consumer voter behavior in the passage of michigan container law. *Journal of Marketing, 45*(2), 19–32.

De Young, R. (1990). Recycling as appropriate behavior: A review of survey data from selected recycling education programs in michigan. *Resources, Conservation and Recycling, 3*, 253–266.

Dolnicar, S. (2010). Identifying tourists with smaller environmental footprints. *Journal of Sustainable Tourism, 18*(6), 717–734.

Dolnicar, S., & Grün, B. (2009). Environmentally friendly behavior: Can heterogeneity among individuals and contexts/environments be harvested for improved sustainable management. *Environment and Behavior, 41*(5), 693–714.

Dolnicar, S., & Leisch, F. (2008). An investigation of tourists' patterns of obligation to protect the environment. *Journal of Travel Research, 46*(4), 381–391.

Fishbein, M., & Ajzen, I. (1975). *Belief, attitude, intention and behavior: an introduction to theory and research.* Reading, MA: Addison-Wesley.

Grunert, S. C. (1991, June). *Everybody seems concerned about the environment: But is this concern reflected in (Danish) consumers' food choice. Special Session at ACR Summer Conference,* Amsterdam.

Hoch, Stephen J., & Deighton, John. (1989). Managing what consumers learn from experience. *Journal of Marketing, 53*(2), 1–20.

Hornik, J., Cherian, J., Madansky, M., & Narayana, C. (1995). Determinants of recycling behavior: A synthesis of recycling results. *The Journal of Socio-Economics, 24*(1), 105–127.

Howenstine, E. (1993). Market segmentation for recycling. *Environment and Behavior, 25*(1), 86–102.

Imran, S., Alam, K., & Beaumont, N. (2014). Environmental orientations and environmental behaviour: Perceptions of protected area tourism stakeholders. *Tourism Management, 40,* 290–299.

Kaiser, F. G., Wolfing, S., & Fuhrer, U. (1999). Environmental attitude and ecological behaviour. *Journal of Environmental Psychology, 19,* 1–19.

Kim, J. (2018). Social dimension of sustainability: From community to social capital. *Journal of Global Scholars of Marketing Science, 28*(2), 175–181.

Kinnear, T., Taylor, J. R., & Ahmed, S. A. (1974). Ecologically concerned consumers: Who are they? *Journal of Marketing, 38,* 20–24.

Lee, H. J., & Park, S. Y. (2013). Environmental orientation in going green: A qualitative approach to consumer psychology and sociocultural factors of green consumption. *Journal of Global Scholars of Marketing Science, 23*(3), 245–262.

Lee, K. (2009). Gender differences in Hong Kong adolescent consumers' green purchasing behavior. *Journal of Consumer Marketing, 26*(2), 87–96.

Lee, Y. K., Kim, S., Kim, M. S., & Choi, J. G. (2014). Antecedents and interrelationships of three types of pro-environmental behavior. *Journal of Business Research, 67*(10), 2097–2105.

Maibach, E. (1993). Social marketing for the environment: Using information Campaigns to promote environmental awareness and behavior change. *Health Promotion International, 8*(3), 209–224.

Martins Gonçalves, H., & Viegas, A. (2015). Explaining consumer use of renewable energy: Determinants and gender and age moderator effects. *Journal of Global Scholars of Marketing Science, 25*(3), 198–215.

Meneses, G. D., & Palacio, A. B. (2005). Recycling behavior: A multidimensional approach. *Environment and Behavior, 37*(6), 837–860.

Miao, L., & Wei, W. (2013). Consumers' pro-environmental behavior and the underlying motivations: A comparison between household and hotel settings. *International Journal of Hospitality Management, 32,* 102–112.

Oliver, J. D., & Rosen, D. E. (2010). Applying the environmental propensity framework: A segmented approach to hybrid electric vehicle marketing strategies. *Journal of Marketing Theory and Practice, 18*(4), 377–393.

Perkins, H. E., & Brown, P. R. (2012). Environmental values and the so-called 'true' ecotourist. *Journal of Travel Research, 51*(6), 793–803.

Rompf, S., Kroneberg, C., & Schlösser, T. (2017). Institutional trust and the provision of public goods: When do individual costs matter? The case of recycling. *Rationality and Society, 29*(2), 160–178.

Schwab, N., Harton, H. C., & Cullum, J. G. (2014). The effects of emergent norms and attitudes on recycling behavior. *Environment and Behavior, 46*(4), 403–422.

Tabernero, C., & Hernández, B. (2011). Self-efficacy and intrinsic motivation guiding environmental behavior. *Environment and Behavior, 43*(5), 658–675.

Vining, J., & Ebreo, A. (1990). What makes a recycler?: A comparison of recyclers and non-recyclers. *Environment and Behavior, 22*(1), 55–73.

Wang, T., Mukhopadhyay, A., & Patrick, V. M. (2017). Getting consumers to recycle NOW! when and why cuteness appeals influence prosocial and sustainable Behavior. *Journal of Public Policy & Marketing, 36*(2), 269–283.

Webster, F. E. Jr. (1975). Determining the characteristics of the socially conscious consumer. *Journal of Consumer Research, 2*(3), 188–196.

Weiner, J. L., & Doescher, T. A. (1991). A framework for promoting cooperation. *Journal of Marketing, 55*(2), 38–47.

Index

Note: The locators in *italics* and **bold** represents figures and tables respectively

For Product Safety Concerns and Information please contact our EU
representative GPSR@taylorandfrancis.com Taylor & Francis Verlag GmbH,
Kaufingerstraße 24, 80331 München, Germany

Printed and bound by CPI Group (UK) Ltd, Croydon, CR0 4YY

08/05/2025

01864358-0017